Living in Christ

Jesus Christ

God's Love Made Visible

Carrie J. Schroeder

saint mary's press

The Subcommittee on the Catechism, United States Conference of Catholic Bishops, has found that this catechetical high school text, copyright 2011, is in conformity with the *Catechism of the Catholic Church* and that it fulfills the requirements of Course II: "Who Is Jesus Christ?" of the *Doctrinal Elements of a Curriculum Framework for the Development of Catechetical Materials for Young People of High School Age.*

Nihil Obstat: Rev. William M. Becker, STD
                 Censor Librorum
                 January 25, 2011

Imprimatur: † Most Rev. John M. Quinn, DD
               Bishop of Winona
               January 25, 2011

The nihil obstat and imprimatur are official declarations that a book or pamphlet is free of doctrinal or moral error. No implication is contained therein that those who have granted the nihil obstat or imprimatur agree with the contents, opinions, or statements expressed, nor do they assume any legal responsibility associated with publication.

The publishing team included Gloria Shahin, editorial director; Jerry Shepherd, contributing author; Lorraine Kilmartin, development editor; Steven McGlaun, consultant; prepress and manufacturing coordinated by the production departments of Saint Mary's Press.

Cover Image: © The Crosiers/Gene Plaisted, OSC

Printed in the United States of America

1143 (PO3750)

ISBN 978-0-88489-904-4, Print
ISBN 978-1-59982-079-8, Digital

Contents

Part 3: Discovering God in Creation 72

Section 3: Jesus:
The Definitive Revelation of God

Part 1: The Incarnation 86

Part 2: The Two Natures of Jesus:
Human and Divine 100

Part 3: Jesus and the Church. .115

Section 4: Jesus: The Definitive Revelation of God's Plan

Section 5: Faith and Our Response to Jesus

Introduction

"Mary of Magdala went and announced to the disciples, 'I have seen the Lord.'" (John 20:18)

How amazing it must have been for Mary of Magdala to proclaim those powerful words of faithful witness on that first Easter morning: "I have seen the Lord!" Sometimes I have wondered: If I had been there at the empty tomb with her, would I have had the challenges to my faith that I have encountered? The people who saw, knew, and talked with Jesus during his earthly ministry witnessed his miracles firsthand and heard his powerful preaching and storytelling with their own ears. Some even saw him alive after he had risen from the dead. Yet we know from Scripture that some of the disciples, like Peter and Thomas, did experience moments of profound doubt. They had been blessed with the privilege of walking with Jesus, knowing him face to face, feeling his touch, and hearing his voice. With that blessing, though, came the task of accepting that the one they had known personally as their teacher, companion, and friend was, in fact, more than all these things: he was the Word become flesh (see John 1:14).

I have come to understand that my own life of faith follows a similar pattern of knowing Jesus yet having moments when my faith is challenged. I have been blessed with the knowledge that Jesus is alive, present, and active in my life, daily offering me strength, grace, wisdom, guidance, and salvation. And yet, to be completely honest, with that blessing comes what is sometimes a hard task, even a struggle: to understand fully what having a relationship with Jesus means. What does it mean for me to say that I, as a member of the Body of Christ, the Church, dwell in a relationship of love, trust, and friendship with Jesus?

One of the ways in which I have tried, throughout my life, to answer that question has been through study. When I was a student in a Catholic high school, my religious studies classes were among my favorites. In high school I finally began to explore not just *what* Catholics believe but *why*; not just how to *read* the Bible but how to *apply* it to my life; and not just what prayer *is* but how to *really pray*. Studying cultivated my faith, and that faith grew stronger the more I learned and put it into practice. After high school I continued to follow a path that I found to be both intellectually and spiritually fruitful: I majored in religious studies in college. When I completed my graduate degree in theology, I began teaching religious studies in a Catholic high school, not unlike the one I had attended years ago. Through these many years, study of Scripture and Tradition has truly helped me to grow in faith in Jesus. It has enabled me to root that faith—including its more affective or emotional aspects—in something solid, something that truly nurtures, challenges, and enlivens my whole self: mind, heart, body, and spirit.

One of the greatest privileges of my life has been to serve as a religious studies teacher and campus minister. In that role I have been delighted by the opportunity to accompany young people, like yourself, on their journeys of faith. I love your exuberant energy, your joy in living, your passion for justice, your challenging spirit, your intellectual curiosity, and your fierce loyalty: these are wonderful gifts you bring to our Church and to our world! If you bring all of these gifts to bear on your study of Jesus this semester, I guarantee that you will not be disappointed. Your efforts will return to you many times over, in the form of greater clarity of belief, deeper trust in God, and a more profound sense of purpose for your life.

This course begins by reflecting on the greatest mystery of our faith, the Trinity: Father, Son, and Holy Spirit. We then look at how God has revealed himself throughout history and most fully in his Son, Jesus Christ. We will see how Jesus reveals to us what it means to be a child of God and how we are to live and act upon our faith.

As you learn about Jesus through this book and in this course, my sincere hope is that your academic work takes deep root in you, opening your mind, touching your heart, and nourishing your soul, so that you may grow and flourish as the person of faith you were created to be. I pray that all your work may draw you more completely into a loving relationship with the one who came that we might have life, and have it more abundantly (see John 10:10). May you, like Mary of Magdala so long ago, see the Risen Lord alive and active, and may you be forever changed by that life-giving encounter.

Wishing you every grace and blessing,
Carrie J. Schroeder

The Trinity

Part 1

God Is One: Father, Son, and Holy Spirit

The faith of Catholics is rooted in the truth that there is one God in three Divine Persons: Father, Son, and Holy Spirit. Belief in one God is called monotheism. Belief that God is three Persons is called Trinitarianism. Trying to understand how Catholics can hold both beliefs is confusing for many people. How is it possible to be both monotheistic and Trinitarian? If God is a Holy Trinity, who are these three Persons? How are they united, and how is each Divine Person distinct? The articles in this part will help you to explore and become knowledgeable about these and other revealed truths about the Holy Trinity.

The topics covered is this part are:

Article 1 God Is One: Catholics Are Monotheistic

The belief in and worship of only one God is called monotheism. Throughout much of human history, people of many cultures have practiced polytheism, which is the belief in many gods. You may have studied some polytheistic cultures, like the ancient Egyptians, Greeks, and Romans, in other courses in school. You may know Hindus or Shintoists who worship many gods. When God began a **covenant** relationship with Abraham, he was revealing an essential truth: there is only one God, the Lord of all the earth. Over time Abraham and Sarah's descendants, who would become known as the Jews, understood and embraced this monotheistic faith.

As Jewish people came to fully understand and embrace this monotheistic faith, they incorporated this belief into their prayer and worship. The Shema, the prayer uttered daily by faithful Jews of ancient times and continuing to the present, begins with these words, found in a slightly different form in Deuteronomy 6:4: "Hear, O Israel, the Lord is our God, the Lord is One" (*Shema Yisrael, Adonai eloheinu, Adonai ehad*). The Bible, in both the Old and New Testaments, consistently reveals that there is only one true God. For instance, in the Gospel of Mark (see 12:28–29), a scribe asks Jesus which is the greatest of all the Commandments. Jesus quotes the words of the Shema. Jesus himself tells us there is only one God.

One God or Three Gods?

When the early Christians first began to understand, speak, and write about the **doctrine** of the **Trinity**, many people thought they were rejecting monotheism in favor of polytheism. Even today praying "in the name of the Father, and of the Son, and of the Holy Spirit" may lead some people to think that Catholics have three gods, not one. Those who mistakenly believe that Catholics worship Mary or other saints may even think we have four or more gods. The *Catechism of the Catholic Church (CCC)* firmly states our belief in one God. "To confess that Jesus is Lord is distinctive of Christian faith. This is not contrary to belief in the One God. Nor does believing in the Holy Spirit as 'Lord and giver of life' introduce any division into the One God" (202).

covenant
A personal, solemn promise of faithful love that involves mutual commitments, such as the sacred agreement between God and his people. In the Old Covenant, God revealed his Law through Moses and prepared his people for salvation. He established a new and eternal Covenant in Jesus Christ, his only Son.

doctrine
An official, authoritative teaching of the Church based on the Revelation of God.

Trinity
The truth that God, although one, is three Divine Persons: the Father, the Son, and the Holy Spirit.

Catholics have always affirmed the truth that God is one. Indeed, we profess this each week at Sunday liturgy when we say the **Nicene Creed**: "[We] believe in one God." ✝

Three Major Monotheistic Religions

Only Christians have recognized God as Trinity—one God in three Divine Persons. However, we share our belief in this one God—and our commitment to **monotheism**—with Judaism and Islam.

The very heart of Judaism is monotheism, as reflected in the Shema, which faithful Jews pray daily. Those who follow Islam, who are known as Muslims, also profess belief in one God. They too proclaim their monotheism as part of their regular prayer. Each day faithful Muslims repeat the *Shahadah*. It is translated:

"There is no God but God and Muhammad is the Messenger of God."

The Second Vatican Council spoke of the "common spiritual heritage" shared by Jews and Christians (*Declaration on the Relation of the Church to Non-Christian Religions* [*Nostra Aetate*, 1965], 4). It expressed dismay for the hatred and persecution Jews have endured at many times throughout history. In this same document, the council expressed "esteem" for Muslims: "They worship God, who is one, living and subsistent, merciful and almighty, the Creator of heaven and earth, who has also spoken to humanity" (3).

To understand what Catholics share with Jews and Muslims does not in any way lessen the truth of our Catholic beliefs. Rather, it helps us to appreciate and marvel at the many people of different times and places who have recognized the reality that there is only one God, Creator of all.

Article 2 God Is Three-in-One: Catholics Are Trinitarian

Do you like a good mystery? Not the crime-solving kind. *Mystery* also means a revealed truth that is beyond our experience and ability to grasp fully. We hold to it by faith but also work to better understand it.

The mystery of the Holy Trinity—the mystery of one God in three Persons—is a unique defining trait of Christian faith. As the *Catechism* states, it is the Church's "most fundamental and essential teaching" (234) and the central mystery of our faith, which only God can fully reveal to us. Every prayer we pray and every Sacrament we celebrate is done in the name of this Triune God—Father, Son, and Holy Spirit.

United, Yet Distinct

The three Divine Persons are inseparable both in what they are and in what they do. "Inseparable in what they *are*"? This means each Divine Person is fully God—complete, whole, and entire. All of God is contained in God the Father. All of God is contained in God the Son. All of God is contained in God the Holy Spirit. "Inseparable in what they *do*"? This means each Divine Person has the same job description, so to speak. Each of the three Persons is engaged in the work of our salvation. Each acts to create us in love, redeem us, and make us holy. As the *Catechism* states, "The whole **divine economy** is the common work of the three divine persons" (258). The work and mission of Father, Son, and Holy

Nicene Creed
The formal statement or profession of faith commonly recited during the Eucharist.

monotheism
The belief in and worship of only one God.

divine economy
Also known as the economy of salvation, this refers to God's eternal plan and his actions for the salvation of humanity.

Pray It!

Blessed Be God Forever!

"Blessed are you, Lord, God of all creation." Do you remember hearing these words at Mass? The celebrant says these words while praying during the Preparation of the Altar and the Gifts. The prayers he says emphasize that it is "through your [God's] goodness" that we have the bread and wine to offer. It is because of God's power that they will become "the bread of life" and "our spiritual drink." The celebrant can say these prayers either aloud or silently. When said aloud, the assembly responds, "Blessed be God forever." Next time you respond with these words at Mass, remember to thank God for the gifts he has already given us and those he will give us.

incarnate
Having become flesh; specifically, God the Son assuming human nature. The Incarnation means that Jesus, the Son of God and Second Person of the Trinity, is both fully God and fully human.

Spirit are inseparable. But "each divine person performs the common work according to his unique personal property" (*CCC*, 258). It was the Son who became Incarnate, assuming a human nature. It is the Holy Spirit who is sent into each believer's heart and is sent to guide the Church.

Even though they are inseparable, the three Persons of the Holy Trinity are truly distinct from one another. This distinction does not divide the divine unity. The Father, Son, and Spirit are in perfect communion with one another.

The three Persons of the Trinity are also distinct in their origins. It is proper to speak of the Father as the generator, even though all three Divine Persons are eternal, existing without beginning or end. We express this Mystery of Faith by saying that the Son is begotten of the Father and that the Holy Spirit proceeds from both the Father and the Son.

If the Persons of the Trinity are united, how are they distinct? First, each carries out the work of our salvation in the way that is most proper. For example, God the Father draws us to follow Christ; God the Son became **incarnate;** God the Holy Spirit gives us the gifts of the Spirit. Second, the three Persons are distinct in their relationship to one another. God the Father is *unbegotten*, meaning he has always existed

Catholic Wisdom

Trinity Sunday

Trinity Sunday, officially known as The Solemnity of the Most Holy Trinity, is celebrated the Sunday after Pentecost. This prayer is from the liturgy for this feast day:

God our Father, who by sending into the world
the Word of truth and the Spirit of sanctification
made known to the human race your wondrous mystery,
grant us, we pray, that in professing the true faith,
we may acknowledge the Trinity of eternal glory
and adore your Unity, powerful in majesty.
Through our Lord Jesus Christ, your Son,
who lives and reigns with you in the unity of the Holy Spirit,
one God, for ever and ever.

(Roman Missal)

without beginning or end. God the Son is *begotten* of God the Father; in the words of the Nicene Creed, "the Only Begotten Son of God, born of the Father before all ages." The Holy Spirit is sent out into the world, *proceeding from* the Father and the Son.

The Trinity Revealed by God in Sacred Scripture

Although the Church did not fully articulate the doctrine of the Trinity until the councils of the fourth and fifth centuries, the presence of the Trinity is clear in Sacred Scripture, especially in the New Testament. For example, in Luke's Gospel, Jesus, "rejoiced [in] the holy Spirit" (10:21), stating that "no one knows who the Son is except the Father, and who the Father is except the Son" (10:22). In the Gospel of John, Jesus says that "whoever has seen me has seen the Father" (14:9). Later in the Gospel of John, just hours before Jesus' death, Jesus prays to God the Father for his disciples, asking "that they may be one just as we are" (17:11). Finally, at the very end of the Gospel of Matthew, Jesus commissions his disciples to baptize "in the name of the Father, and of the Son, and of the holy Spirit" (28:19). These and other passages help us to understand that the God revealed to us in Scripture is a Trinity of Divine Persons. ☩

© kwest/shutterstock.com

The mystery of the Trinity is revealed in the Scriptures and Tradition. How would you explain this mystery to someone who has never heard of it?

"In the name of the Father . . ."

© Oscar C. Williams/shutterstock.com

"In the name of the Father, and of the Son, and of the Holy Spirit. Amen." Have you ever thought about how often you have said these words while making the Sign of the Cross? Hundreds of times? thousands? How often have you reflected on what these words and gesture really mean?

Everything Catholics do is done in the name of the Trinity. Most notably, every Catholic has been baptized in the name of the Father, and of the Son, and of the Holy Spirit. When we begin our personal and communal prayer in this way, including our celebrations of the Eucharist and other Sacraments, we recall that by the grace of Baptism, we are to share in the life of the Blessed Trinity. Maybe you make the Sign of the Cross before a difficult test or before you go to sleep. The Sign of the Cross helps us to remember—in both word and action—who we are: God's beloved children, living always under the love, protection, and guidance of the Blessed Trinity.

The next time you make the Sign of the Cross, make sure you aren't mumbling the words under your breath or making the motion in haste. Make both the words and the gesture a bold proclamation of your faith in the Triune God.

3 The First Person of the Trinity: God the Father

filial

Having to do with the relationship of a child to his or her parents.

If the Holy Trinity is three Divine Persons, who are these three Persons? The First Person of the Trinity is God the Father, the Eternal Source of all that exists. As we profess in the Nicene Creed, the First Person of the Trinity is the "maker of heaven and earth, of all things visible and invisible." Many religions, including Judaism, have understood God as Father, reflecting that God is the Creator and Lord of all the earth. When we profess that God is our Father, we acknowledge that he is the source of all life; that all creation exists because of God. Further, we acknowledge that God is all-powerful and desires to be in an intimate, loving relationship with his creation. He loves us, cares for us, provides for us, heals us, forgives us, and is just and faithful. Even if the love of an earthly father—or mother, or friend, or any other person—disappoints us, God's faithful love will never, ever fail us.

Jesus Reveals God the Father

In the Gospels, Jesus calls God *Abba,* which, in his native language of Aramaic, means "Father." This reveals two things about his relationship with God the Father:

- Jesus' relationship with God was **filial,** a father-son relationship. In prayer Jesus knew his Father's unconditional love, strength, and guidance. But even more important, Jesus reveals a new way of understanding God as Father—as the First Person of the Trinity, the Eternal Father of the Eternal Son.

- Jesus' relationship with God the Father is an intimate one. In Jesus' prayer we see him speaking to his Father directly and personally, revealing his inner thoughts and feelings (see Matthew 11:25–26 and Mark 14:36). Jesus also teaches about God the Father in his parables. For example, in the parable commonly known as the Prodigal Son (see Luke 15:11–32), Jesus tells the story of a father who loves both of his sons with patience, compassion, and joy. If you have never read this story, read it now. It is a clear glimpse, given to us by Jesus, of the gentle, transforming love of God the Father.

beatitude
The state of eternal happiness with God in Heaven.

We Are God's Adopted Children

Jesus does more than teach about his loving Father. He actually invites us to call God "Father" ourselves. In doing so Jesus invites us into the close relationship he has with his Divine Father—into the communion of the Holy Trinity. Through Baptism we become God the Father's adopted daughters and sons. As Saint Paul writes: "You received a spirit of adoption, through which we cry, '*Abba*, Father!' The Spirit itself bears witness with our spirit that we are children of God, and if children, then heirs, heirs of God and joint heirs with Christ" (Romans 8:15–17).

This does not mean that God cares for us only if we are baptized. On the one hand, "the Church does not know of any means other than Baptism that assures entry into eternal **beatitude**" (*CCC*, 1257). On the other hand, we believe that God's infinite love and tender mercy extend to all people, even in ways we cannot fully understand. ✞

Live It!

God Is a Loving Parent

When we call God "Father," we are reminded that we are his children. This means we are blessed with a heavenly Father who loves and cares for us. It means we have a loving Father we can always turn to. God is a great parent who wants to listen and provide support. He is always there no matter our mood or situation. We can tell him about triumphs, defeats, hopes, and fears. We can ask for help, advice, or forgiveness.

Have you ever talked with God as if you were talking with a loving parent? For the next three days, write down three or four things each day that happen to you. It could be as simple as "I got an A on a test," "Volleyball practice was hard today," or "I was really lonely at lunch." Spend time going through the list and talking with God about each item. Tell him what is going on in your life, and thank him for being with you.

Is God Male?

The answer to that question is a most definite no. To say that God is our Father is to talk about the First Person of the Trinity, the Father of the Eternal Son, who has adopted us as sons and daughters. It does not mean God is a human being. It certainly does not mean God is literally male. Both Judaism and Christianity have always maintained that God has no gender. In other words, God is neither male nor female. Jesus affirms this in his conversation with a Samaritan woman when he asserts that "God is Spirit" (John 4:24). The *Catechism* reminds us that God has characteristics we associate with both fathers and mothers when it states: "God's parental tenderness can also be expressed by the image of motherhood,[1] which emphasizes God's immanence, the intimacy between Creator and creature. . . . We ought therefore to recall that God transcends the human distinction between the sexes" (239).

Both the Old and New Testaments use a great variety of symbolic images when speaking about God. Some of these are masculine images, like "the LORD, your God, carried you, as a man carries his child, all along your journey" (Deuteronomy 1:31). Others are feminine images. Jesus tells a parable about a woman searching for a lost coin (see Luke 15:8–10). The woman represents God, who patiently searches for us when we are "lost" in sin. Others are neither masculine nor feminine, like Psalm 19, which describes God as "my rock" (19:15). Praying with many scriptural images helps us to deepen our relationship with God. It reminds us that no human language can ever fully capture or describe the Divine Mystery.

4 The Second Person of the Trinity: God the Son

Article

The Second Person of the Trinity is God the Son, who assumed a human nature for our salvation. Jesus Christ is both truly and fully God and truly and fully human. He has a unique relationship with God the Father: he is the only, and the Eternal, Son of God.

Jesus Is Truly God

Several New Testament passages may help us to understand that Jesus is truly God, who became flesh through the power of the Holy Spirit. For example, the prologue to John's Gospel states:

> And the Word became flesh
> and made his dwelling among us,
> and we saw his glory,
> The glory as of the Father's only Son,
> full of grace and truth.
>
> (1:14)

John's Gospel also contains another often-quoted line about the purpose of the Incarnation: "For God so loved the world that he gave his only Son, so that everyone who believes in him might not perish but might have eternal life" (3:16). In his Letter to the Philippians, Saint Paul says this of Jesus:

> . . . though he was in the form of God,
> did not regard equality with God
>   something to be grasped.
> Rather, he emptied himself,
> taking the form of a slave,
> coming in human likeness;
> and found human in appearance.
>
> (2:6–7)

These and other Scripture passages, as well as the writings of the early Church councils, help us to understand that Jesus Christ is the Son of God—a title that signifies his unique and eternal relationship with God the Father. He is truly God's own self made flesh among us.

Jesus Is Truly Human

Jesus is not only truly and fully God but also truly and fully human. He is not only the Son of God but also the Son of Mary. As Saint Paul writes in his Letter to the Galatians: "When the fullness of time had come, God sent his Son, born of a woman, born under the law" (4:4). Jesus Christ has a fully human nature. So, he is able to teach us, through his words and actions, how to be the best, most authentic people we can be. Specifically, Jesus teaches us to love one another— even our enemies—as God the Father has loved him and as he has loved us. He teaches us to love the truth, to pray always in faith, and to forgive those who have wronged us. By assuming human nature, Jesus has shown us how to live in a way that reflects the fullness and beauty of God's Reign.

Last Judgment
The judgment of the human race by Jesus Christ at his second coming, as noted in the Nicene Creed. It is also called the Final Judgment.

Why Did God Become Incarnate?

The name Jesus, given to him by the angel Gabriel, means "God saves" in Hebrew. This tells us that the Incarnation is part of salvation history: God's eternal plan to redeem and save humanity. The *Catechism* states that God became incarnate for the following four reasons (457–460):

- to save us by reconciling us with God
- to share divine love with us
- to show us how to be holy
- to enable us to share in God's divine nature

Athanasius, a fourth-century saint, says that "the Son of God became man so that we might become God,"[2] or share in God's divine life (460). That is good and amazing news indeed! At his Ascension, Jesus' humanity entered into God's heavenly domain, from where he will come again at the **Last Judgment.**

The Nativity is a reminder of the Incarnation. Why do you think God chose to enter the world in the form of an infant born in a manger?

© Peter Zelei/istockphoto.com

Messiah
Hebrew word for "anointed one." The equivalent Greek term is *christos.* Jesus is the Christ and the Messiah because he is the Anointed One.

Pentecost
In Sacred Scripture, the event in which the early followers of Jesus received the Holy Spirit. Today the Church celebrates this event on Pentecost Sunday, which occurs seven weeks after Easter Sunday.

Christ: Not Jesus' Last Name

Because the Second Person of the Trinity is often referred to as Jesus Christ, some people mistakenly think that Christ is Jesus' last name. *Christ* is a title given to Jesus, based on the Greek word *christos*, which means "anointed one." The Hebrew equivalent is **Messiah**. In the ancient world, anointing with oil symbolized being chosen by God for some special mission or purpose. For example, in the Old Testament, priests, prophets, and kings were anointed as they prepared to undertake their new role in the community. In the case of Jesus, he is "anointed by the Holy Spirit, from the beginning of his human existence" (*CCC*, 486), anointed to be our Savior and Redeemer. ✞

Article 5 The Third Person of the Trinity: God the Holy Spirit

The Third Person of the Trinity is the Holy Spirit. In the words of the Nicene Creed, the Holy Spirit is "the Lord, the giver of life, who proceeds from the Father and the Son." The Holy Spirit has been active since the time of Creation, speaking to God's people through the ancient prophets and anointing Jesus for his special mission to redeem and save us.

The Father, Son, and Holy Spirit are distinct Persons, but they are inseparable from one another. From the beginning of time until the end of time, wherever the Father sends his Son, he also sends his Spirit. They share a joint mission to bring us into the Body of Christ as God's adopted sons and daughters. However, the Holy Spirit was not fully revealed until after Jesus' death and Resurrection.

Promised by Jesus, Given at Pentecost

In John's Gospel, when Jesus knows that the hour of his death is near, he promises his disciples that he will ask God to send them an advocate (in Greek, *paraclete*). An advocate is someone who is on our side, to help us, strengthen us, and empower us for holiness. This advocate Jesus promises is the Third Person of the Holy Trinity. Jesus explains that the Spirit will teach the disciples everything they need to know.

After Jesus dies and rises, he makes good on his promise. The Risen Lord appears to the disciples, breathes on them, and says, "Receive the holy Spirit" (John 20:22). Moreover, at **Pentecost,** he sends the Holy Spirit, now fully revealed, to be with his disciples forever—both those who were his earliest followers and we who are his followers today. The Acts of the Apostles describes Pentecost in this way: "Suddenly there came from the sky a noise like a strong driving wind, and it filled the entire house in which they were. Then there appeared to them tongues as of fire, which parted and came to rest on each one of them. And they were all filled with the holy Spirit" (2:2–4).

Receiving the gift of the Spirit means that the mission of Jesus becomes the mission of the Church. In fact, it becomes *our* mission. The Spirit empowers us to follow the way of Jesus by sharing God's love with our friends and families, being a healing presence to those in need, and preaching the Good News through our words and actions. Because Jesus is no longer physically present here on earth, the Paraclete blesses and strengthens our efforts to live as Jesus did: bringing justice, peace, and truth to all those we meet. ✝

The Gifts of the Holy Spirit	
Wisdom	opens our eyes to see God at work, even in our common, everyday experiences.
Understanding	makes it possible for us to follow the correct course of action in difficult or confusing situations.
Counsel	also called right judgment, helps us to know right from wrong and to choose the good consistently.
Fortitude	or courage, enables us to do the right thing, even when we are afraid.
Knowledge	empowers us to use our intellectual abilities to learn more about our faith.
Piety	or reverence, reminds us that God is God, and we are not. With the gift of reverence, we recognize that all we are, all we do, and all we have comes from God.
Fear of the Lord	also called wonder and awe, fills us with a spirit of profound respect as we marvel at God's power and goodness.

The Holy Spirit Makes *Us* Holy

The Holy Spirit sanctifies the People of God by offering us seven gifts to help us as we strive to live as Christians. Look at the chart on page 23 that describes the Gifts of the Holy Spirit and think about these questions:

- Of these gifts, for which are you most grateful?
- Which do you find most difficult to understand?
- Which do you need the most?

Part Review

1. What is monotheism?

2. What three major religions are monotheistic?

3. What does it mean that the three Divine Persons are united? What does it mean that they are distinct?

4. What evidence do the Scriptures offer for the existence of the Trinity?

5. What do we acknowledge when we profess that the First Person of the Trinity is Father?

6. In the Gospels what does Jesus reveal to us about his relation to the Father?

7. What four reasons does the *Catechism* give for the Incarnation?

8. What is the role of the Holy Spirit as the advocate for Christians throughout time?

9. What are the seven Gifts of the Holy Spirit?

Part 2

The Development of Trinitarian Doctrine

Have you ever studied something that you know is true but found it took a lot of effort to try to understand and explain it? The Mystery of the Trinity is like that.

For even the most thoughtful theologian, the most distinguished philosopher, or the holiest saint, the Trinity is a complex reality to grasp and express. God revealed the truth of our Trinitarian faith to the very earliest Christians, but it took time for the Church to clarify the depths of this truth. In fact, it took several centuries for early bishops and Church Fathers to develop and agree on language that would best express the subtle nuances of one God in three Divine Persons.

During these early centuries of Church history, varied ideas about the Trinity existed, especially about Jesus' place in it. The early Church sifted through all these ideas—some correct and some incorrect. Their efforts bore fruit in the early Ecumenical Councils. These Councils produced the Nicene Creed and other clear statements of core Catholic truths. They shaped the language and direction of Trinitarian theology for centuries to come.

The topics covered is this part are:

6 The Early Church Faces Challenges to Apostolic Faith

After Jesus died, rose, and ascended to Heaven, the early Church faced the enormous task of precisely articulating the doctrine about the Trinity and about Jesus and defending those truths against those who challenged them. During these first centuries, bishops and **Church Fathers** worked at these tasks. They often did so in official gatherings called **Ecumenical Councils.** They developed the language that would reflect, as fully as possible, the depth, breadth, and meaning of these sacred, revealed truths.

Many people had their own theories about who Jesus was and what his time on earth had achieved. Many of these ideas were heresies, or false teachings. This complicated the early Church's task. She was kept very busy defending the true teachings passed on from the Apostles when so many conflicting and false theories were circulating.

The Early Church Develops Trinitarian Language

In his Second Letter to the Corinthians, Saint Paul writes: "The grace of the Lord Jesus Christ and the love of God and the fellowship of the holy Spirit be with all of you" (13:13). This very early New Testament letter was written in the mid-50s AD. It shows the early Church's firm belief in the Trinity from the earliest times. However, it is one thing to know something is true; it is quite another thing to speak and write about that truth in a way that will make sense to other people. To express the doctrine of the Trinity, the Church Fathers turned to the language of **philosophy.** This language, though

Church Fathers
Teachers and writers in the early Church, many of whom were bishops, whose teachings are a witness to the Apostolic Tradition.

Ecumenical Council
A worldwide gathering of Catholic bishops convened by the Pope to discuss and resolve issues and problems the Church is facing.

philosophy
In Greek this word literally means "love of wisdom." It refers to the study of human existence using logical reasoning.

Catholic Wisdom

The Words of Saint Irenaeus

"The Church, having received this preaching and this faith, although scattered throughout the whole world, yet, as if occupying but one house, carefully preserves it. She also believes these points just as if she had but one soul, and one and the same heart, and she proclaims them, and teaches them, and hands them down, with perfect harmony, as if she possessed only one mouth."

often difficult for us to understand, was in common use at that time. Paragraph 252 of the *Catechism* explains the following words, which are used to describe Trinitarian doctrine:

- The word *substance* is used to name "the divine being in its unity."
- The word *person* (in Greek, *hypostasis*) is used to refer to the Father, Son, and Holy Spirit, each fully God, yet each distinct.
- The word *relation* is used to indicate that the distinction among the three Persons lies in the relationship of each to the others.

Developing this standard vocabulary in speaking and writing about the Trinity was a great help to the Church Fathers. They could more easily express the faith of the early Christian community and defend that faith to those who challenged it. ♱

Saint Irenaeus, Defender of the Faith

Saint Irenaeus was a second-century bishop in what is now Lyons, France. As a prolific writer, he was a key figure in the many controversies that developed as the early Church sought to clarify her Trinitarian faith. His most famous work is a series of books called *Against Heresies*. In it Irenaeus stresses how crucial it was for the Church to safeguard her apostolic faith. This was the faith that Jesus had shared with the Apostles and that they had passed on to their successors. Irenaeus is particularly concerned about Gnosticism. This was one of the false teachings about Jesus that was circulating in the Church at that time. Irenaeus's courageous effort to defend apostolic faith against Gnosticism and other heresies can inspire us. We too need to speak the truth without fear, trusting always in God's steadfast love.

Saint Irenaeus's feast day is June 28.

By the Hand of Nicholas P. Papas, Greensburg, PA

7 Early Christological Heresies

Article

How can 100 percent man and 100 percent God equal 100 percent Jesus? That just doesn't seem to add up! The mystery of Jesus' being fully human and fully divine doesn't make sense as math or science. The early bishops and Church Fathers struggled to articulate and defend this Mystery of Faith against errors and misinterpretations. This is because during the first several centuries of the Church, some **Christological** heresies, or incorrect beliefs about Jesus, developed.

Christology
Literally the study of Christ; the systematic statement of Christian beliefs about Jesus Christ, including his identity, mission, and saving work on earth.

Focusing on Jesus' Humanity Only

Have you ever debated with someone who was so convinced he or she was right that he or she completely lost sight of the truth on the other side? Player X, for them, is the best, so player Y has no value. Something like that happens with the heresies about Jesus.

Some heresies downplayed or denied the divinity of Jesus. For example, Arianism claimed that Jesus was created, just as we were. Arius, its proponent, said that Jesus did not exist before he was conceived in Mary's womb. Arius believed that Jesus was a higher creature than humans but less than God. Nestorianism believed that in Jesus there were actually two Persons. One was divine and one was human. Nestorius argued that it was wrong to say things like "God suffered and died for us" or "God was born of the Virgin Mary." These statements would apply to the human person Jesus, but not to the Divine Person. Nestorius was really concerned about stressing the humanity of Jesus. He would not even allow the Virgin Mary to be known as the Mother of God.

Focusing on Jesus' Divinity Only

Other heresies played down the humanity of Jesus. Docetism alleged that Jesus' humanity was a sort of disguise—he looked like a human and acted like a human, but inside, he was really just God. For example, Docetists claimed that Jesus didn't really suffer on the cross. They said he *appeared* to be suffering, but he couldn't *really* suffer a human death because he was God. Monophysitism believed that Jesus' divinity fully absorbed his humanity, so that, in the end, he was only divine and not human.

The name Gnosticism comes from *gnosis*, the Greek word for "knowledge." It was a series of religions, common in the Greco-Roman world. It claimed that salvation can be reached only by getting special, secret knowledge from God

Heresies Focusing on Jesus' Humanity	
Name	Belief
Arianism	Jesus was created, just as we were, and he did not exist before he was conceived in Mary's womb. Jesus was a higher creature than humans but less than God.
Nestorianism	In Jesus there were actually two Persons, one divine and one human. It was improper to say statements that would apply to only the human person Jesus, not the divine Person.

Heresies Focusing on Jesus' Divinity	
Name	Belief
Docetism	Jesus' humanity was a sort of disguise—he looked like a human and acted like a human, but inside he was really just God.
Monophysitism	Jesus' divinity fully absorbed his humanity, so that, in the end, he was only divine and not human.
Gnosticism	Salvation can be attained only by acquiring special, secret knowledge from God or God's agent.

Pray It!

Prayer for Sharing the Truth

Jesus Christ, Son of God and Son of Mary,
Sharing your truth with the world can be difficult and intimidating. Help us to speak and act in accord with your teaching. Guide us in treating all of your children with respect, care, and understanding. Inspire us to overcome any anxiety we might have in sharing your Good News with the world. Teach us to befriend, pray, and sacrifice so that all may know your truth.

Loving God, strengthen us in times we falter and struggle in sharing your Good News. Help us to always remember that you embrace us in your love and forgiveness.
Amen.

or God's agent. The Christian form of Gnosticism said that Jesus was not a man at all, but a semidivine being. God sent him to share this special knowledge with a select, elite group of people God wanted to save.

The Church Defends the Truth

These Christological heresies caused a great deal of division within the Church. Most of the heresies were incorrect teachings about either Christ's human nature or his divine nature. Because of all of this controversy, the Church Fathers needed to present the doctrine of the Incarnation in clear, careful, and balanced teaching. We can benefit from their writings

Mary, Mother of God: The *Theotokos*

The Catholic Church's teachings and beliefs about Jesus are closely related to her teachings and beliefs about his mother, Mary. As early as the New Testament period, Mary was revered as the Mother of Jesus. However, she did not receive the title Mother of God until the Nestorian heresy was renounced at the Ecumenical Council of Ephesus in 431. This Council affirmed Mary as the *Theotokos*, a Greek word that literally means "God-bearer" but is often translated as "Mother of God." Today both the Roman Catholic Church and the Eastern Orthodox Churches continue to venerate her with this title. Honoring Mary as the *Theotokos* acknowledges the unique role she played in our salvation. She brought the presence of God into the world in a way no one else could. Because she is the Mother of Jesus, she is also the Mother of God.

How can you bring God's presence into your home, school, and other activities? Let Mary's example of faith and courage motivate and empower you to carry God's life, love, and grace to a world in great need of healing and hope.

today. They are easily available to those who take the time to find them. The Incarnation is truly a mystery, but that does not mean it is completely beyond our understanding. Rather it is a Mystery of Faith because its truth is so deep that we can never exhaust everything that it has to teach us. ✝

Article 8 The Ecumenical Councils of the Early Church

Throughout the Church's history, bishops have met in gatherings called Ecumenical Councils to discuss the challenges facing the Church. A particular focus of the Ecumenical Councils in the early centuries of the Church was the challenges to Christological and Trinitarian doctrines. Between AD 325 and AD 787, seven Ecumenical Councils were held. We will discuss the two most important of these; both took place in ancient cities located in modern-day Turkey.

The Council of Nicaea

In AD 325 the Council of Nicaea declared that Jesus is truly God. In technical language, it declared that God the Son is "of the same substance" as God the Father. Stating and defending this belief countered the heretical claims of Arianism, which maintained that Jesus was more than human but less than God—a sort of "in-between" creature.

The Council of Nicaea also produced the first draft of what is now known as the Nicene Creed. You may be familiar with this Creed from praying it at Sunday liturgy. It states

Ecumenical Councils of the Early Church

Location	Year	Outcome
Council of Nicaea	325	the Nicene Creed
Constantinople	381	revised the Nicene Creed by adding the clauses referring to the Holy Spirit
Ephesus	431	defined the true personal unity of Christ and declared Mary the Mother of God (Theotokos)
Chalcedon	451	defined the two natures of Christ (divine and human)

that Jesus is "born of the Father before all ages, God from God, Light from Light, true God from true God." These lines, written nearly seventeen hundred years ago, continue to express, with both beauty and clarity, Jesus' identity as the Second Person of the Trinity.

The Council of Chalcedon

Whereas the Council of Nicaea focused on understanding the Trinity, especially the relationship and distinction between God the Father and God the Son, the Council of Chalcedon focused on understanding the inner life of God the Son. In

The Second Vatican Council

Not all Ecumenical Councils are part of ancient history. In fact, the Church has continued to hold Ecumenical Councils from time to time throughout her history. Ecumenical Councils are convened by the Pope, the successor to Saint Peter and the Vicar of Christ, or are at least confirmed or recognized by him. The Pope must confirm the decisions made during the Council.

The most recent Ecumenical Council was the Second Vatican Council, convened by Pope John XXIII and held from 1962 to 1965. Sometimes it is referred to simply as Vatican II. This Council issued sixteen documents dealing with a variety of topics, including the liturgy, Christian education, religious freedom, and the relationship of the Church to non-Christian religions. Many of the decisions made at Vatican II continue to affect the spiritual lives of Catholics today.

Periodically holding Ecumenical Councils, synods, and other gatherings is a sign of the Church's willingness to explore pressing needs and issues. She wants to respond to these concerns with the message, values, and truth of the Gospel.

solemnities
Important holy days in the Catholic liturgical calendar, such as Christmas, Easter, Pentecost, and All Saints' Day.

other words, what is the relationship between Jesus' humanity and his divinity? In the year 451, the 350 bishops attending the Council of Chalcedon declared that Jesus' two natures (his human nature and his divine nature) are undivided and inseparable. Jesus is 100 percent human and 100 percent divine. He is not half man and half God; nor is he two Persons somehow pushed into one. Jesus, God the Son, is *one* Divine Person with *two* natures. As the *Catechism* states, quoting a document produced by the Council of Chalcedon, Jesus is "consubstantial with the Father as to his divinity and consubstantial with us as to his humanity"[3] (467). ✝

Article 9 The Nicene Creed

Chances are you've studied the Declaration of Independence already. Part of it sums up what people in the British colonies of North America believed in 1776 about their civil rights. A creed does something like that also. A creed is a summary statement of the beliefs of an individual or a community. The creed most Catholics are familiar with is the Nicene Creed. The formal name for this creed is the Niceno-Constantinopolitan Creed. It is the product of two Ecumenical Councils—the Council of Nicaea held in AD 325 and the Council of Constantinople in AD 381, at which it was promulgated.

Proclaiming Shared Beliefs

Catholics say the Nicene Creed at Sunday celebrations of the Eucharist as well as at **solemnities,** Baptisms, and other special liturgical celebrations. This recitation of the Creed during a liturgy is called the profession of faith. Saying the Creed together in this way allows the gathered assembly to "respond to the word of God proclaimed in the readings taken from Sacred Scripture and explained in the homily and that they may also call to mind and confess the great mysteries of the faith" (*General Instruction on the Roman Missal*, 67). It also underscores our unity as one community of faith. We can help and support one another in our efforts to be faithful to the truths we profess together. Moreover, because we belong to a global Church, we are united in faith, through the Creed, with Catholics throughout the world.

The Creed and Baptism

From the early centuries of the Church, the Creed has played an important role in the liturgy of Baptism. Because Baptism is the Sacrament by which one becomes a Christian, it was important for the people being baptized to know and profess the beliefs of the community they were joining. Most Catholics today were baptized as babies, so our parents and godparents promised to raise us according to the faith of the Church as stated in the Creed. Thus, praying the Creed each Sunday is a way for us to dedicate ourselves again to the Catholic faith. We renew our commitment to the promises made by us, or by others on our behalf, at our Baptism.

Key Concepts in the Nicene Creed

Even if you are familiar with the Nicene Creed, take the opportunity to read it carefully now and find where it expresses these key doctrines of our faith:

- The Creed expresses a Trinitarian faith in God the Father, God the Son, and God the Holy Spirit.
- The Creed identifies Jesus' birth, death, Resurrection, and Ascension as key events in our salvation.
- The Creed states the four "marks" or characteristics of the Church: the Church is One, Holy, Catholic, and Apostolic.
- The Creed affirms belief in the resurrection of the dead and in the Last Judgment.

© Francesco Maria Cura'

When we pray the Nicene Creed, we renew our baptismal promises. Read the Creed on page 36. Identify what it states about the three Divine Persons of the Trinity and the Church.

The core truths of the Church expressed clearly and concisely, in a way that invites prayer, reflection, and further study—this is the wisdom and the appeal of the Nicene Creed. ✝

The Nicene Creed

I believe in one God,
the Father almighty,
maker of heaven and earth,
of all things visible and invisible.

I believe in one Lord Jesus Christ,
the Only Begotten Son of God,
born of the Father before all ages.
God from God, Light from Light,
true God from true God,
begotten, not made, consubstantial
    with the Father;
through him all things were made.
For us men and for our salvation
he came down from heaven,
and by the Holy Spirit was incarnate
    of the Virgin Mary,
and became man.

For our sake he was crucified under
    Pontius Pilate,
he suffered death and was buried,
and rose again on the third day

in accordance with the Scriptures.
He ascended into heaven
and is seated at the right hand of the
    Father.
He will come again in glory
to judge the living and the dead
and his kingdom will have no end.

I believe in the Holy Spirit, the Lord,
    the giver of life,
who proceeds from the Father and the
    Son,
who with the Father and the Son is
    adored and glorified,
who has spoken through the prophets.

I believe in one, holy, catholic and
    apostolic Church.
I confess one Baptism for the
    forgiveness of sins
and I look forward to the resurrection
    of the dead
and the life of the world to come.
Amen.

Article 10 The Trinity: Model for Human Relationships

What does the Trinity have to do with you? For many Catholics the Trinity can seem like an incomprehensible mystery, a distant reality, or an abstract theory. In fact, the Trinity isn't unrelated to our human experience. The *Catechism* tells us that "there is a certain resemblance between the unity of the divine persons" (1890) and the kind of relationships we should have with one another.

What is this "certain resemblance"? How should our human relationships reflect what we see in the Trinity? The Trinity is a dynamic communion of Persons who dwell together in love and unity. They never cease to reach out with grace, compassion, and mercy to all humanity. Our Triune God is not distant from us, unconcerned with our joys and struggles; rather, our God is involved in human history. Our God is so involved, in fact, that he became part of human history through the Incarnation of Jesus Christ.

This is the God in whose image we are created, and this is the God with whom we are destined to live forever in Heaven. While we live on earth, we are to live like this God— in relationship with others, not in isolation. As the *Catechism* states, through "exchange with others, mutual service and dialogue"[4] (1879), we grow as people, discover our gifts and talents, and learn to live in the way God wants. In this way the Trinity, as a communion of Divine Persons, gives us a foundation for relationships built on unity, truth, and love.

How can you use the Trinity as a model for your own relationships?

Live It!

Take Time to Listen

How can we live a Trinitarian life, in communion with God and with others? How can we grow in that "mutual service and dialogue" (*Catechism*, 1879) that God wants for us as sharers in his life and love? Building upon our baptismal grace that unites us in love with God—Father, Son, and Holy Spirit—we can work toward mutual respect and love toward one another. Mutual respect and love require that we take time to listen.

Listening is not always easy. If you sense a conversation will be difficult, pray first. Ask the Holy Trinity for help in seeing the other person as a child of God and a brother or sister in Christ. Ask the Holy Spirit to help you to listen.

Then focus on the person speaking and give your full attention. Try not to think of what you might say in return. Eliminate distractions—such as a cell phone or TV. If you don't understand something, ask questions. Make eye contact.

When it is time for you to respond, ask the Holy Spirit to guide you to speak with love and to provide the advice, encouragement, or support the other person needs.

- You can be involved in the lives of your family members, even when it is inconvenient.
- You can reach out to a new student at your school.
- You can enlarge your circle of friends and acquaintances to include people that others may have overlooked or excluded.
- You can take on a new role or ministry in your parish community.

Can you think of other ways?

When we live out our call to community in these and other ways, we are truly following God's design. That design is revealed for us in the Mystery of the Holy Trinity: three Persons living forever in unity and love as One. ✝

God created us to live as a part of a community, supporting, serving, and loving one another. How do you support, love, and serve those in the communities of your family, school, church, and city?

Part Review

1. What difficult tasks did the early Church face in safeguarding the apostolic faith?

2. What were the two main types of heresies about Jesus in the early Church?

3. Why do we use the title "Mother of God" to refer to Mary?

4. What did the Council of Nicaea declare about Jesus? What belief about Jesus was the Council defending?

5. What did the Council of Chalcedon affirm about the relationship of the human and divine natures in Jesus?

6. Why do Catholics say the Nicene Creed at certain liturgical celebrations?

7. What are some of the key doctrines of the Catholic faith that the Nicene Creed states?

8. In what ways can the Trinity be a model for human relationships?

Revelation

Part 1

The God-Human Relationship

We believe that God has been engaged in a loving relationship with us since the beginning of human history. He has planted in our hearts the desire to be united with him and has freely offered us the gift of Revelation. Through the life, death, and Resurrection of Jesus Christ, he has saved and redeemed us through the power of the Holy Spirit. When you respond to God in faith, you yourself become a part of this great drama of salvation history.

Responding to God with wholehearted faith can be challenging at times. Although he freely offers us the gifts of faith and reason, we still find ourselves confronted with difficult, complex questions. For example, we may wonder if God really exists. We may question why he doesn't seem to be doing anything about all the suffering and evil in the world. The resources of our Catholic faith can help us to probe difficult questions like these as we seek to respond in love to the God who first loved us.

The topics covered is this part are:

- Article 11: "What Is Revelation?" (page 42)

- Article 12: "Sharing in God's Life" (page 45)

- Article 13: "Salvation History" (page 47)

- Article 14: "How Do We Know God Really Exists?" (page 50)

- Article 15: "Evil and Suffering and a Good and Powerful God" (page 53)

Article 11 What Is Revelation?

salvation history
The pattern of specific events in human history in which God clearly reveals his presence and saving actions. Salvation was accomplished once and for all through Jesus Christ, a truth foreshadowed and revealed throughout the Old Testament.

Have you ever wanted to get to know someone better? How do you do this? You might really listen to what the person says and watch what the person does. To really get to know someone means that the person has to share who she or he is in words and deeds. That is what God has done and continues to do throughout salvation history.

Revelation is God's self-disclosure to us. Self-disclosure means that God gradually reveals himself and the divine plan of salvation to humanity through deeds and words. God offers "an enduring witness to Himself in created realities" (*Dogmatic Constitution on Divine Revelation* [*Dei Verbum*, 1965], 3). This means we can learn about God in the events and experiences of our daily lives, the order and beauty of the natural world, the lives of the saints and other believers, and the wondrous abilities of our human intellect and reason. But God further reveals a type of knowledge that we would not be able to grasp on our own.

Revelation Is a Gift

Revelation is a loving gift offered to us, not something that God needs to provide. The *Catechism of the Catholic Church (CCC)* refers to God's "utterly free decision" (50). To be known by us and to give himself to us, he freely chooses to share his Divine Self with us. This allows us to know God more fully than we ever could on our own. Revelation also empowers us to respond to him with love and devotion. The more you know God, the more you will love him.

How Does Revelation Occur?

Revelation of the divine plan, which also discloses much about who God is, has unfolded slowly, in stages, throughout **salvation history.** The Old Testament tells the story of how God, over many centuries, reached out to our ancestors in faith—Abraham, Sarah, Moses, and David, for example. Over time God formed his people into a holy nation. He spoke to them through the prophets Isaiah, Jeremiah, and Amos, among many others. The New Testament tells the story of God's final and full Revelation in the Person of Jesus

Doctors of the Church

When someone refers to doctors, you might first think of people with a medical degree. But the word *doctor* comes from the Latin verb *docere*, meaning "to teach." It can refer to those who are well qualified to teach. The Catholic Church has recognized thirty-three theologians with the title Doctor of the Church. Theologians are scholars who study the history and teachings of the Church as their life's work. All the Doctors of the Church were not only theologians but also saints. They were individuals whose lives showed great holiness in the service of God and his people. The Doctors of the Church help us through the witness of their lives and the wisdom of their theological writings. They guide us in understanding and interpreting the Revelation of the divine plan in salvation history.

The first four Doctors of the Church were designated in 1295 by Pope Boniface VIII. They were Saint Ambrose (pictured below), Saint Augustine, Saint Jerome, and Saint Gregory the Great. The three Doctors of the Church named most recently have all been women. In 1970 Pope Paul VI honored Saint Catherine of Siena and Saint Teresa of Ávila with this title. Pope John Paul II bestowed the same honor on Saint Thérèse of Lisieux in 1997.

Christ, the incarnate Word of God and Son of the Father. Today the Holy Spirit continues to empower the Church to interpret and shed light on the mystery of God's Revelation. In this way, over many centuries, God revealed the divine plan of loving goodness.

In Jesus Christ, Revelation is complete. There is nothing that we need to know for our salvation that wasn't revealed through Jesus' life, teachings, Passion, death, and Resurrection. God's people will continue to grow in understanding of what he has revealed, but there won't be new public Revelation until his plan is fulfilled.

We Cannot *Fully* Know God

If Revelation is complete in Jesus Christ, does that mean we've got God "all figured out"? Unfortunately, no. Though having answers to our many questions about God might sound appealing, we cannot *fully* know him during our earthly lives. Even with the benefit of Revelation, God is beyond our limited human capacity for thought, words, speech, and understanding. As the *Catechism* states, quoting Saint Augustine, a fourth-century bishop: "God remains a mystery beyond words: 'If you understood him, it would not be God'" (Saint Augustine, *Sermo* 52, 6, 16: J. P. Migne, ed. Patrologia Latina [Paris: 1841–1855] 38:360 and *Sermo* 117, 3,5: J. P. Migne, ed. Patrologia Latina [Paris: 1841–1855] 38, 663) (230). Even though we cannot *fully* know God while we live on earth, we can certainly experience divine love and mercy when we attune our minds, hearts, and spirits to the many signs of God's active, loving presence in the world. ✝

For Saint Augustine, his mother, Saint Monica, was a sign of God's active and loving presence in the world. Who or what is a sign of God's love for you?

Article 12 Sharing in God's Life

Revelation makes it possible for humanity to respond to God's plan of loving goodness for us. What is God's plan for us? It is to live in communion with him, to have a share of God's own life, to love as God loves. God has planted in our hearts the desire for him; through Revelation this divine-human bond becomes clear.

We Are Made for God

Human beings are, "by nature and **vocation**," religious beings because we are "coming from God" and "going toward God" (*CCC*, 44); "the desire for God is written in the human heart" (27). In other words, we have been created to be in communion with God. We have a built-in longing to be a part of this bond between humanity and divinity.

As evidence for this, the *Catechism* points to the many "prayers, sacrifices, rituals, meditations" (28) that are key parts of nearly every human culture. In fact, most of the world's people, in all places and in all times, have believed in, worshipped, and sought out the Divine. This is not a coincidence; rather, it is a sign that we reach the fullness of our humanity only when we heed this built-in bond with our Creator.

God Calls Us to Fullness of Life

God would not place the desire for him within our hearts and then leave us to our own devices to figure out how to reach God. Rather, God has reached out to humanity over and over again throughout history, seeking to connect with us in mutual love. From the very beginning of time, through the age of the **patriarchs,** through the time of the Exodus, and through the era of the Israelite kings and prophets, God has revealed himself. His self-disclosure has been fulfilled in the Incarnation of the Divine, Eternal Son, Jesus Christ. The Incarnation is the ultimate work of Divine Revelation. Jesus' saving mission shows us how much God loves us by God's becoming one of us in order to save us. In the Letter to the Ephesians, Saint Paul writes of this "plan for the fullness of

vocation
A calling from God to fulfill a particular purpose or mission in life.

patriarchs
The ancient fathers of the Jewish people, whose stories are recounted in the Book of Genesis.

times, to sum up all things in Christ, in heaven and on earth" (1:10). The Second Vatican Council explains it this way:

> Jesus perfected revelation by fulfilling it through his whole work of making Himself present and manifesting Himself: through His words and deeds, His signs and wonders, but especially through His death and glorious resurrection from the dead and final sending of the Spirit of truth. (*Divine Revelation*, 4)

Saint Augustine of Hippo

The life of Saint Augustine of Hippo demonstrates how God never fails to seek us out, even when we are lost, confused, or burdened.

Saint Augustine was born in AD 354 in North Africa. In his young adulthood, he followed a Persian religion called Manichaeanism. During this time he fathered a child with a woman who was not his wife. At the age of thirty-two, Augustine felt drawn to reading the New Testament, and he resolved to be baptized as a Christian. He was later ordained a priest and named Bishop of Hippo, in North Africa, a post he held until his death in AD 430.

Saint Augustine's spiritual autobiography, *The Confessions*, is considered a classic of western literature. As he reviewed his life in the pages of the book, he clearly saw the hand of God at work, even though he had been unaware of it at the time. He especially perceived God's presence in the love, concern, and prayers of his mother, Saint Monica. Saint Augustine realized that even when he was lost in sin, God's plan was slowly unfolding in his life. God had never stopped searching for him. Speaking to God in his book, he wrote, "You have made us for yourself, and our heart is restless until it rests in you."

Today in the ministry and Sacraments of the Church, God continues to offer friendship. In Baptism we become adopted daughters and sons of the Divine Father, as we enter into the life and death of Jesus. When we participate in the Eucharist, we share in the sacrifice of Jesus, the Son. When we take part in these Sacraments, and when we engage in prayer and reflection on the Scriptures, we do so through the power of the Holy Spirit. We are not acting on our own initiative; rather, we are responding, in faith, to the promptings placed in our hearts by the Triune God. ✝

Article 13 Salvation History

The first and universal witness to God's love is creation itself. If we are open to it, creation makes known to us a loving, caring, and wise God who wants to be in loving union with all his creation, especially human beings. When human sin threatened God's purpose for creation, God responded with a plan for our salvation, a plan that culminates in his new creation in Christ Jesus.

God's plan to save us from sin and death occurs within history, not outside it. In other words, God acts *within* historical events. He uses both the events of the world and the events of our own daily lives to redeem and save humanity. We call the unfolding of God's plan for us salvation history. Salvation history began at the dawn of the universe and continued through all the events of the Old Testament. It culminated in the life, death, and Resurrection of Jesus. The fullness of God's loving plan for humanity will be revealed at the end of time.

The Promise of the Old Testament

The Old Testament tells the story of God's loving relationship with all humanity—beginning with the family of Adam and Eve. God created us to live in communion with him and thus find our happiness. Even when Adam and Eve sinned by disobeying God—an event known as the Fall—their Creator did not abandon them. Rather, God "buoyed them up with the hope of salvation, by promising redemption" (*Divine Revelation,* 3). As salvation history continued to unfold, God established a covenant with Noah and, later, with the ancient Israelites.

The history of ancient Israel began with God's call to Abraham to leave his and his wife Sarah's homeland and to become the ancestors of God's Chosen People:

> I will make of you a great nation,
>   and I will bless you;
> I will make your name great,
>   so that you will be a blessing.
>   (Genesis 12:2)

Abraham and Sarah's grandson Jacob had a large family, consisting of two wives—Rachel and Leah—twelve sons, and one daughter. When Israel became a nation, the Twelve Tribes would be named for these twelve sons of Jacob.

When the Israelites later became enslaved in Egypt, God brought them to freedom through the leadership of Moses, aided by his brother, Aaron, and his sister, Miriam. At Mount Sinai, God formed a new covenant with the Israelites and revealed the Law. This covenant is often called the Sinai Covenant or the Mosaic Covenant.

As salvation history continued, God called kings and priests to be the Israelites' political and religious leaders. God also sent prophets to call them back to fidelity when they sinned. The prophets offered them the hope of a new and everlasting covenant: "I will place my law within them, and write it upon their hearts" (Jeremiah 31:33).

Pray It!

Lesson from Abraham

When we hear about Abraham's relationship with God, we might be tempted to say, "I wish God would speak to me directly and tell me what he wants me to do with my life." God might not come to your house and sit down at the table to tell you what he wishes for you, but God continues to speak to each one of us. We just have to be willing to listen. Some of the ways we listen to God include praying, being active in our parishes, attending Mass, and reading Sacred Scripture.

Be ready! When you take the time to listen to God, you might be challenged like Abraham to make dramatic changes in your life. As he said to Abraham, God is saying to you, "Fear not . . . / I am your shield; / I will make your reward very great" (Genesis 15:1).

Through these many centuries, God never ceased to share mercy, love, and grace with the people of Israel. They never ceased to be God's Chosen People, "the first to hear the Word of God"[1] (*Catechism*, 839).

Jesus Christ, the Savior of the World

The Revelation of God's loving plan in history finds its fulfillment in the Incarnation. In the words of the Letter to the Hebrews, "In times past, God spoke in partial and various ways to our ancestors through the prophets; in these last days, he spoke to us through a son" (1:1–2). Indeed, what better way to reveal the divine plan to us than by becoming one of us? The life, death, and Resurrection of Jesus—the Eternal Son of God made flesh—is God's definitive effort to save us, to reveal the truth, and to bring us to the fullness of life. ✝

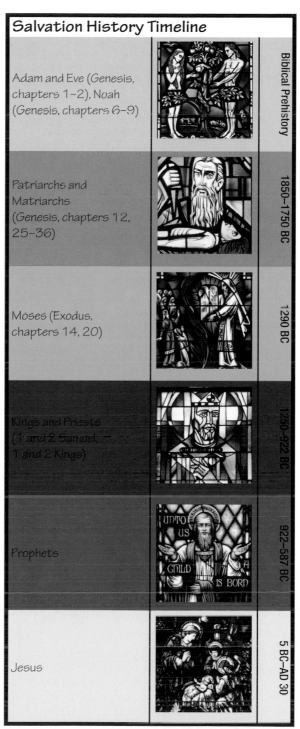

Salvation History Timeline

Adam and Eve (Genesis, chapters 1–2), Noah (Genesis, chapters 6–9)		Biblical Prehistory
Patriarchs and Matriarchs (Genesis, chapters 12, 25–36)		1850–1750 BC
Moses (Exodus, chapters 14, 20)		1290 BC
Kings and Priests (1 and 2 Samuel, 1 and 2 Kings)		1250–922 BC
Prophets		922–587 BC
Jesus		5 BC–AD 30

Images in the chart above © The Crosiers/Gene Plaisted, OSC

Article 14 How Do We Know God Really Exists?

If you have ever wondered whether God really exists, you are not alone. This question has captivated the imaginations of the greatest religious thinkers of many generations. It can be hard to accept something we can't see with our eyes, and trusting in a spiritual reality requires self-surrender. We don't believe in God only because it makes good sense to do so; rather, we believe because he is trustworthy (see *CCC*, 156). Nevertheless, he has given us several sources that can help to assure us of his existence.

Sacred Scripture: The Witness of an Inspired Text

In the Gospels, Jesus sends the Twelve Apostles on a mission: "He summoned the Twelve and gave them power and authority over all demons and to cure diseases, and he sent them to proclaim the kingdom of God and to heal [the sick]" (Luke 9:1–2). After Jesus' death and Resurrection, these Twelve Apostles—with many other disciples as their coworkers—continued this mission. They preached the Good News of God's Reign through their words and actions. Eventually the witness of these very early followers of Jesus—those people who had been commissioned by Christ himself—was preserved in the writings of the New Testament. The New Testament is a rich and varied collection of Gospels, epistles, sermons, speeches, parables, and accounts of miracles. Because it was written through the inspiration of the Holy Spirit, it is a privileged place for us to encounter God's strong, reliable, and active presence.

Other Believers: The Witness of Faith-Filled Lives

The testimony of those with a strong belief in God can inform our own approach to the question of God's existence. God offers the same gift of faith to all people, but sometimes we hear of people who have responded to that gift with extraordinary trust despite trials, suffering, and persecution. Their stories are especially powerful. The fact that so many people—both in ancient times and quite recently—have been willing to die as **martyrs** for their Christian faith can challenge us to reconsider our own doubts. Could all these people have been mistaken?

Not only martyrs lead faith-filled lives. Many of us are blessed with living examples of people whose unshakable faith deepens our own sense of God's reality. You might think of parents, grandparents, and other family members, as well as teachers, priests, and deacons. All of these can give us the desire and the motivation to root our lives more firmly in faith.

martyrs
People who suffer death because of their beliefs. The Church has canonized many martyrs as saints.

Reason and Conscience: The Witness of God's Gifts Within Us

The *Catechism*, quoting Saint Anselm, states that "faith *seeks understanding*"[2] (158). This means that though faith is a sure and certain gift of God, we are able to use our human faculties to understand our faith more fully. Indeed God created us with human reason and a moral conscience. God wants us to use these gifts to explore our religious questions, including the question of his existence. When we truly listen to the message inherent in creation and to our conscience, we discover that God "can be known with certainty from the created world by the natural light of human reason"[3] (*CCC*, 36). In other words, our brains and our faith are not on parallel tracks that will never intersect. Our reason and intellect can nourish our faith in God's existence, for "a more penetrating knowledge will in turn call forth a greater faith" (158).

Try to bring these different sources—Sacred Scripture, the witness of other believers, and human reason—to your prayer. They will help you to truly grow in your knowledge and experience of God. This does not mean you will never

Catholic Wisdom

Aim in Life

At Auschwitz death camp, someone once asked Saint Maximilian Kolbe whether his sacrifices for others "made sense in a place where every man was engaged in a struggle for survival." He answered: "Every man has an aim in life. For most men, it is to return home to their wives and families, or to their mothers. For my part, I give my life for the good of all men" (Blessed Maximilian, OFM, Conv.).

doubt God's existence again. Such questions and concerns are normal and natural parts of the human condition. It does mean you will have the resources to investigate your questions with honesty, clarity, and humility. ✝

Saint Maximilian Kolbe of Auschwitz

Death camps. Gas chambers. Crematoria. The mass annihilation of eleven million human beings. How would it be possible to believe in God's existence amidst the unspeakable horror of the Holocaust?

Saint Maximilian Kolbe was born in Poland in 1894. He was ordained a Franciscan priest as a young man. When Hitler invaded Poland in 1939, Kolbe spoke out against Nazi oppression. He protected Jews from persecution. His arrest in 1941 brought him to Auschwitz, the largest of the Nazi killing centers—camps established for the specific purpose of mass murder.

One day, after some prisoners tried to escape from the camp, ten men were chosen at random to be starved to death. One of the ten, Franciszek Gajowniczek, protested that he had a family who would be devastated by his death. In a courageous act of Christian faith, Kolbe volunteered to take Gajowniczek's place and was sent to the starvation bunker. When he was found still alive after ten days with no food or water, he was killed by lethal injection.

Gajowniczek survived Auschwitz and lived to be ninety-four years old. Kolbe had an unwavering faith in Jesus. It led him to literally give his life so that another could live.

Saint Maximilian Kolbe's feast day is August 14. He trusted in the reality of God's love, mercy, and protection even in the worst circumstances imaginable. His example can strengthen our own desire to believe.

^{Article} 15 Evil and Suffering and a Good and Powerful God

Fire, famine, and earthquakes. Violence, disease, and war. If God is all powerful and all good, how can there be so much suffering in the world? Human attempts to answer this age-old question are called theodicy. In many ways the whole Christian story seeks to answer this question: *"There is not a single aspect of the Christian message that is not in part an answer to the question of evil"* (CCC, 309). Within that Christian story, let's consider four key elements of the Church's theodicy.

The World Is Yet Imperfect

Our world is far from perfect. This should be obvious to anyone who turns on a television or glances at a newspaper. First, natural disasters like floods, droughts, and earthquakes continue to happen throughout the world. These events are not punishment from God or a sign of divine anger or displeasure; they are simply part of the laws of nature. The more perfect exists alongside the less perfect for now, until God's ultimate plan for the world is fully revealed. The *Catechism* explains it this way: "With infinite wisdom and goodness God freely willed to create a world 'in a state of journeying' toward its ultimate perfection" (310).

Second, human beings continue to sin and commit evil acts. Because God created us with **free will,** we have the option to sin. God respects our freedom. He never forces us to choose the good, even though suffering for ourselves or others often results when we sin. This means we continue to live in an imperfect world. However, by learning to use our free will wisely, we participate in God's work of spreading the **Reign of God** throughout the world.

Redemptive Suffering

Because Jesus' death redeemed, or saved, humanity from sin, we view suffering, especially when endured on behalf of others, as redemptive. Because God suffered in the Person of Jesus, he is truly with suffering people in a very special way. Our suffering unites us with the crucified Christ, and our

free will
The gift from God that allows us to choose between good and evil. Human freedom attains its perfection when directed toward God. It is the basis for moral responsibility.

Reign of God
The reign or rule of God over the hearts of people and, as a consequence of that, the development of a new social order based on unconditional love. The fullness of God's Reign will not be realized until the end of time. Also called the Kingdom of God.

efforts to alleviate the suffering of others allow us to serve the very Body of the Crucified Lord.

The Paschal Mystery

The Church's theodicy is rooted not only in Jesus' death on the cross but also in his Resurrection. Because we were baptized into Christ's death, we will share in his Resurrection: we also will live again after we die. The Resurrection is not just about life after death. It is also about the Paschal Mystery, the centerpiece of Christian faith. The Paschal Mystery shows us that suffering, sin, and evil will never have the last word. Just as God brought the hope and joy of the empty tomb out of the agony and torment of the cross, so will he bring forth new life and hope out of the most desperate and seemingly hopeless situations today.

We See Only Partially

Our good and gracious God always wills and desires what is best for humanity. It is easy to believe this when life is good. Suffering reminds us that we cannot see the "big picture" that God can see. Experiences of pain and loss challenge us to trust that "all things work for good for those who love God" (Romans 8:28). At these times we are invited to place our confidence in God's plan for human history, even

Live It!

Dealing with Setbacks

How well do you unite sufferings in your personal life with Jesus' example of redemptive acts of love? Smaller setbacks probably afflict you with annoying regularity. A test you expected to ace goes badly. A date you were sure you'd get doesn't happen. A game you hoped to win proves a disaster. You can either mope or offer these frustrations up in prayer. You might even find that they make you more humble, responsible, and compassionate.

Sometimes larger sufferings blindside you. A friend moves away or betrays you. A major illness flattens you or someone you love. Financial or other difficulties damage your family. Afflictions test your faith and commitment to God. Can you accept what the Father allows, unite yourself with Jesus' cross, and hope in the value of the suffering? The struggle may be hard, but Jesus' Resurrection gives us the hope we need to keep going.

though it is difficult for us to understand why suffering must be a part of that plan. "Faith gives us the certainty that God would not permit an evil if he did not cause a good to come from that very evil, by ways that we shall fully know only in eternal life" (*CCC*, 324). Suffering and evil are never good in themselves, but the powerful love and mercy of our God can transform the worst suffering or the deepest evil into something good.

In his First Letter to the Corinthians, Saint Paul contrasts the perspective on life we have now, while we are on earth, with the clearer, more complete view we will have in Heaven. He writes: "At present we see indistinctly, as in a mirror, but then face to face. At present I know partially; then I shall know fully, as I am fully known" (13:12).

Encounters with suffering and evil are difficult and distressing. Still, we can trust that somehow, in a way we cannot yet fully understand, the hand of God is at work. God is bringing the world to the state of perfection for which it was created. ✝

Natural disasters, such as Hurricane Katrina, are an unfortunate part of our lives. When we are grounded in our faith, we have the strength to persevere and have our suffering transformed into something good.

© Alex Neauville/shutterstock.com

Part Review

1. If we can know about God through our own reason and observation, why did God make Revelation available to us?

2. Throughout history humans have been seeking God. Why do we have that inborn tendency?

3. What is salvation history?

4. In what ways is God's loving plan in history fulfilled in the Incarnation?

5. What sources of information can help to assure us that God really exists?

6. Given that faith is a sure and certain gift of God to believe in him, why should we try to use our reason to reach him?

7. What is theodicy? What are the key elements of the Catholic approach to theodicy?

Part 2

Sacred Scripture and Tradition

God created us in love and redeemed us in mercy. He offers us numerous opportunities to grow in holiness through meaningful encounters with revealed truth. Both the Old and New Testaments of the Scriptures offer wisdom and opportunities to strengthen our faith as they recount the stories of God's covenant love, first with the ancient Israelites and later with the Church. Tradition, the process of sharing and passing on all that God has communicated, also offers us paths to holiness. Both Scripture and Tradition point us to Jesus Christ, the Word of God, who is the complete and final Revelation of God.

Some people wonder whether this Deposit of Faith—that is, the truth revealed by God through Scripture and Tradition—could really have a divine origin. The Church, however, has faithfully preserved and shared the truth of Christ's original mission with generations of believers from the apostolic age to the present. This assures us that God indeed dwells in and with the Church, inviting us to share in the fullness of life.

The topics covered is this part are:

- Article 16: "God's Revelation through Sacred Scripture: The Old Testament" (page 58)

- Article 17: "God's Revelation through Sacred Scripture: The New Testament" (page 60)

- Article 18: "God's Revelation through Tradition" (page 63)

- Article 19: "Passing On God's Revelation" (page 65)

- Article 20: "The Lives of the Saints" (page 68)

inspired

Written by human beings with the guidance of the Holy Spirit to teach without error those truths necessary for our salvation.

Gentile

Someone who is not Jewish.

Article

16 God's Revelation through Sacred Scripture: The Old Testament

The Old Testament recounts the story of God's covenant relationship with the ancient Israelites. Through this collection of sacred, **inspired** writings we learn the gradual process of God's self-disclosure to humanity, which ultimately points to the fullness of God's Revelation in Jesus Christ. The Old Testament communicates great wisdom and insight as it reveals God's saving plan.

A Lasting Sign of God's Love

Christians "read the Old Testament in the light of Christ crucified and risen" (*CCC,* 129). This does *not* mean that the life, death, and Resurrection of Jesus Christ made the Old Testament out of date or no longer needed. "The Old Testament is an indispensable part of Sacred Scripture. Its books are divinely inspired and retain a permanent value"[4] (121). As Saint Paul wrote, "The gifts and the call of God are irrevocable" (Romans 11:29). To put it another way, God is always faithful. His relationship with the ancient Israelites, who today are known as Jews, endures forever. God's commitment to Abraham and all his descendants, even to the present day, will never end. Thus, the inspired books of the Old Testament—which contains books that are also the Sacred Scripture of the Jewish people—will always be a privileged way for people of faith, both Jews and Christians, to encounter God.

The Roots of Christianity

Christians enrich their faith lives through familiarity with the stories, characters, and themes of the Old Testament because Christianity is rooted in Judaism. Think of the image of a family tree. The family begins at the base of the tree trunk. Then it grows in many directions, represented by the branches. Saint Paul used this very image to show the relationship between Judaism and Christianity. Writing to **Gentile** Christians, he said, "You . . . have come to share in the rich root of the olive tree. . . . Consider that you do not support the root; the root supports you" (Romans 11:17–18).

The Old Testament in Catholic Liturgy

Did you know that about half of the readings from Sacred Scripture proclaimed at Sunday Eucharistic liturgies are taken from the Old Testament?

At a typical Sunday Mass, Catholics hear four readings. Two are usually from the Old Testament—the first reading and the psalm. The first reading is chosen to fit in with the theme or focus of the Gospel reading on that particular Sunday. For example, think of the reading from John's Gospel in which Jesus promises "living water" to a Samaritan woman. It is paired with a reading from the Book of Exodus in which Moses miraculously brings forth water from a rock in the desert. As we pray and worship with a pair of readings like this, the Old Testament helps us to come to a deeper understanding of God's Revelation, which is brought to fulfillment in Jesus Christ, the focus of the New Testament.

The psalm is usually sung rather than read. That's why many people forget that it is actually a biblical text. The Book of Psalms is often called the prayer book of ancient Israel. It has also been a cornerstone of Christian prayer for many centuries.

The next time you go to Mass, pay careful attention to the readings from Sacred Scripture. What is God revealing in both the Old Testament reading and the Gospel proclamation? What psalm is sung? What new insights into Judaism, Christianity, and the person of Jesus do these ancient texts offer you?

In Saint Paul's analogy, Judaism is the original tree; the Gentile Christian communities are the branches that were grafted onto the tree. Just as a transplanted branch could never survive without the support of the original tree's root, Christianity grows from the roots of Judaism.

Understanding the Old Testament as the root of our Christian faith also reminds us that Jesus, as a member of a Jewish family, would have grown up studying the Old Testament and learning its stories. Joseph and Mary would have taught Jesus about the patriarchs, Moses and the Law, and the kings and prophets. The story of God's covenant love with ancient Israel became a part of Jesus' identity and mission. Thus, study of the Old Testament gives Christians great insight into the person and saving work of Christ himself. ✝

Article 17 God's Revelation through Sacred Scripture: The New Testament

The Old Testament tells the story of God's saving work among many generations of ancient Israelites. It shows his covenant relationship with them. In contrast, the New Testament covers a much shorter period of time. It focuses on the saving life and work of one person: Jesus, the Eternal Son, sent by the Father to redeem us in the Holy Spirit.

The Life and Teachings of Jesus

You've probably read books about the lives of famous people you admire. Maybe they were sports stars or actors or other celebrities. Maybe they did great deeds or helped large numbers of people. But the most amazing story of all, a real must-read, is about Jesus Christ, true God and true man.

All of the New Testament writings are rooted in the historical life and teachings of Jesus of Nazareth. Jesus was born as a baby, grew up as a member of the Holy Family, and began his public ministry as an adult. If these events had not occurred, there would not be a New Testament. Although the New Testament is not a complete, biographical account of the life of Christ, it does faithfully transmit "all that Jesus did and taught until the day he was taken up" (Acts of the Apostles 1:1–2).

Oral Tradition

Many people are surprised to learn that none of the New
Testament writings was composed while Jesus was alive. For
probably twenty years after Jesus' death and Resurrection,
little, if anything, was written about him. Instead, his disciples shared their experience of Jesus through oral tradition,
or "word of mouth." They even traveled to distant cities in
the Roman Empire to share what was already being called
the Good News—the Gospel—of Jesus Christ: the fulfillment of God's saving plan. The travels of these early believers are called the missionary campaign because these people
witnessed to their faith in Jesus and encouraged others to
join them.

The Epistles

The earliest writings of the New Testament were the epistles,
or letters; the first were written by Saint Paul beginning
around the year AD 51. Saint Paul had encountered the
Risen Lord in a vision on the road to Damascus. He was
the most famous person to join in the missionary campaign
in the decades just after Jesus' death and Resurrection.
He traveled to cities like Corinth, Thessalonica, Philippi,
and Rome. After leaving those cities for new missionary
destinations, he wrote letters to the Christian communities
he had left behind. These letters are preserved in the
New Testament. They offer us marvelous insights into
the early Church and the faith that led Saint Paul and his
coworkers to take incredible risks for the sake of the Gospel

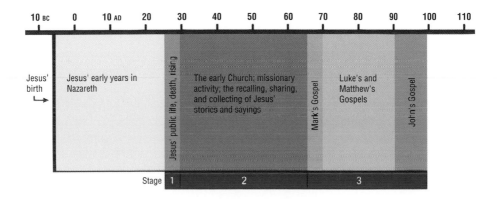

Evangelists
Based on a word for "good news," in general, anyone who actively works to spread the Gospel of Jesus; more commonly and specifically, the persons traditionally recognized as authors of the four Gospels, Matthew, Mark, Luke, and John.

canon of Scripture
The list of the books of the Bible officially recognized as sacred, inspired writings.

noncanonical
Writings that are not part of a canon.

message. Try to study and pray with these deep, often very moving, writings. It will deepen your understanding of the redemptive work of Christ.

The Gospels

Around the year AD 70, the first Gospel, Mark, was written. It was followed by the Gospels of Luke, Matthew, and finally John, which was probably written around the year AD 95. The Gospels are not a complete record of the life of Jesus; in other words, they are not biographies. The **Evangelists** wrote for certain early communities. They chose the teachings, parables, and miracles of Jesus that would be most useful for nurturing the faith of the communities for whom they were writing. As the Vatican II document *Divine Revelation* states, "The sacred authors, in writing the four Gospels, selected certain of the many elements which had been handed on, either orally or already in written form; others they synthesized or explained with an eye to the situation of the churches" (19). The texts they wrote—the four Gospels—have always been treated with a special reverence by Christians. As *Divine Revelation* explains: "It is common knowledge that among all the inspired writings, including those of the New Testament, the Gospels have a special place, and rightly so, because they are our principal source for the life and teaching of the incarnate Word, our Saviour" (18). ✝

Catholic Wisdom

Paul's Journeys

Saint Paul undertook four missionary journeys that took him to numerous towns and cities in Greece and the region we know as the Middle East. His fourth journey was from Jerusalem to Rome. He was arrested in Jerusalem and sent to Rome for trial and eventually execution. Chapters 21– 28 of the Acts of the Apostles recount this dramatic story, which includes a near riot, a shipwreck, and a miraculous snakebite.

Canon Formation

The collection of seventy-three books that make up the Bible is called the **canon of Scripture.** Twenty-seven of these are the books of the New Testament. These twenty-seven were not the only writings about Jesus that were around during the years after his death and Resurrection. Many other writings—including other books on the life of Jesus Christ—claimed to be authentically inspired texts. The early Church Fathers determined which books formed the canon of the New Testament based on three criteria:

- The writer was an Apostle or close associate of an Apostle.
- The writing was used by many different church communities in their prayer and worship.
- The content reflected and supported the Church's beliefs about Jesus' identity and mission.

The **noncanonical** writings are not a secret. There has been no Church conspiracy to keep them under wraps. However, because they were not inspired by the Holy Spirit, they do not reflect true teachings about Jesus and can mislead the uninformed.

Article 18 God's Revelation through Tradition

Some Christians mistakenly rely on only Scripture for God's Revelation. Catholics, however, recognize the authority of both Scripture and Tradition. Scripture and Tradition both come from God, so they are not separate or contradictory. Rather, they are two ways of transmitting Divine Revelation.

What Is Tradition?

Are there stories your family enjoys that have been told over and over again? Some of them may be from years ago. Maybe they concern how your great-grandparents came to this country or how your parents first met. Something like this happens with accounts of God's actions in the Church.

In Jesus Christ, the Eternal Son, God the Father revealed himself to humanity. He entrusted this Revelation to the Apostles. Christ commanded the Apostles to preach the Gospel to the ends of the earth; to share the fullness of

Magisterium

The official, authoritative teaching voice of the Church.

Tradition

This word (from the Latin, meaning "to hand on") refers to the process of passing on the Gospel message. Tradition, which began with the oral communication of the Gospel by the Apostles, was written down in Scripture, is handed down and lived out in the life of the Church, and is interpreted by the Magisterium under the guidance of the Holy Spirit.

his revealed truth so that all might be saved (see Matthew 28:19–20). Inspired by the Holy Spirit, the Apostles did this, in both preaching and writing. The Apostles' teaching authority was passed on to the popes and bishops who succeeded them (the **Magisterium**) so that the apostolic teaching would be handed on to all generations until Christ comes again in glory. This living transmission of the Good News of Jesus Christ is called **Tradition,** or sometimes the Apostolic Tradition. It is distinct from Sacred Scripture. Consider this order of events to better understand the process of Tradition:

- The Apostles witness Jesus' life, teachings, death, and Resurrection. Jesus charges them to share this Good News (which can also be called Revelation, the Word of God, or the Gospel) with all people. In the Jewish Scriptures (which will become the Old Testament), they see many stories and prophecies pointing to Christ, which they now understand more clearly.

- Inspired and strengthened by the Holy Spirit, the Apostles first share the Good News with those people to whom they preach.

- Later the Apostles and others write about the Good News in the form of Gospels and letters.

- These writings become the New Testament canon.

- Through the centuries until the end of time, the Magisterium interprets and teaches the Word of God to the whole world.

Each step of this process is guided by the Holy Spirit. The bishops, in communion with the Pope, give "an authentic interpretation of the Word of God, whether in its written form or in the form of Tradition"[5] (*CCC,* 85).

The Unity of Tradition and Scripture

Because Tradition and Scripture are both "flowing from the same divine well-spring" (*Divine Revelation,* 9), they are working together to achieve the same goal. The Second Vatican Council identified Tradition and Scripture as the two primary ways the Church passes on God's revealed truth: "Sacred Tradition and sacred Scripture make up a single sacred deposit of the Word of God, which is entrusted to the Church" (*Divine Revelation,* 10). Together they hand down the Gospel. They both reveal God to us, so we must respect both: "Both Scripture and Tradition must be accepted and honored with equal devotion and reverence" (*Divine Revelation*, 9). ♱

Tradition versus tradition?

Is that a capital *T* or a small *t*? *Tradition* with a capital *T* is the process of passing on God's authoritative Revelation in the Church. Tradition is a *living* process. This means it is ongoing and never ending, because new generations always need to hear the Gospel message.

In contrast, *tradition* with a small *t* refers to a custom. Do you sing "Silent Night" at Christmas midnight Mass? wear a medal of your patron saint? pray the Rosary during the month of October? These are traditional Catholic customs. They are not part of God's authoritative Revelation, so they can be changed or altered to suit different circumstances, time periods, and cultures. In other words, if "Silent Night" is a *tradition*—rather than part of *Tradition*—it would be okay to sing a different song at Christmas Mass.

Article 19 Passing On God's Revelation

You may have wondered how we can be sure the beliefs and teachings of the Church come from God. How do we know that someone didn't just make up all this? Understanding Apostolic Succession and papal infallibility can help us with this question.

Apostolic Succession

The Church teaches today the same Word of God that Jesus entrusted to his Apostles. When Jesus chose the Apostles, he commissioned them to share in his ministry of preaching the truth and proclaiming the Reign of God. As we read in Mark's Gospel, Jesus "went up the mountain and summoned those whom he wanted and they came to him. He appointed twelve [whom he also named apostles] that they might be with him and he might send them forth to preach and to have authority to drive out demons" (3:13–15). Jesus called

ecumenism

The movement to restore unity among all Christians, a unity that is a gift of Christ and to which the Church is called by the Holy Spirit.

interreligious dialogue

The Church's efforts to build relations with *other world religions,* such as Judaism and Islam.

these Apostles to share in his mission during his earthly life. He also commissioned them to continue it after his death, Resurrection, and Ascension (see Matthew 28:16–20). They, in turn, shared the mission that Christ had entrusted to them with their designated successors, who passed it on to their successors, and so forth, even to the present day. In this way the truth that Jesus shared with the first Apostles continues to be preached today through their successors. This process is called Apostolic Succession.

The Pope, who is the Bishop of Rome, and all the bishops of the Church, are the modern-day successors of the Apostles. Vatican II's *Dogmatic Constitution on the Church* (*Lumen Gentium,* 1964) states this clearly: "The apostolic tradition is manifested and preserved throughout the world by those whom the apostles made bishops and by their successors down to our own time" (20). Christ continues to teach through the Magisterium, the official teaching authority of the Church. In this way he keeps his promise to the Apostles. He is with us until the end of time (see Matthew 28:20).

Infallibility

In order to guarantee that his followers in every time and place would continue to have access to the truths necessary for salvation, Christ has given the Church a share in his own infallibility. The doctrine of papal infallibility was held by the faithful for many years, but it was formally declared at the First Vatican Council in 1870. *Infallible* means "without error." This teaching means that statements of the Pope are true in certain situations. The Pope is infallible when "he proclaims by a definitive act a doctrine pertaining to faith or morals"[6] (*CCC,* 891). The Pope is *not* speaking infallibly every time he makes a remark about the weather! Rather, the Holy Spirit guides the Pope and keeps him from error when he speaks *ex cathedra* about matters essential to our salvation. Literally, *ex cathedra* means "from the chair." It tells us that the Pope is speaking in his official role as authoritative teacher.

What about individual bishops other than the Pope? They cannot speak infallibly by themselves, but the *whole body* of bishops (which includes the Pope) can share in the gift of teaching infallibly on matters of faith and morals.

The Catholic Church and Other Religions

Doctrines such as Apostolic Succession and papal infallibility can be hard for non-Catholics to understand. Despite this, it is important to seek unity among Christians and with all people of good will, without compromising the truths of faith. In recent years the Catholic Church has made huge strides in building bridges with other Christians and with people of other faiths.

- The Vatican II *Decree on* **Ecumenism** (*Unitatis Redintegratio*, 1964) stressed that the Sacrament of Baptism unites all Christians: "All who have been justified by faith in baptism are incorporated into Christ" (3).

- Also among the writings of Vatican II is the *Declaration on the Relation of the Church to Non-Christian Religions* (*Nostra Aetate*, 1965). It speaks of the "high regard" in which the Catholic Church holds other faiths. These often "reflect a ray of that truth which enlightens all" (2).

- The late Pope John Paul II built on the views expressed at Vatican II. He began **interreligious dialogue** with the Jewish community. He was the first Pope since Saint Peter to visit a synagogue. He was also the first Pope to pray at the Western (Wailing) Wall in Jerusalem (pictured below).

- Pope Benedict XVI has continued to visit Jewish communities throughout the world. He has also dialogued with Muslims.

Efforts to dialogue with people of other religions do not alter or water down the Catholic Church's mission to pass on God's revealed truth. Rather, these ecumenical and interfaith efforts are an essential part of our mission. We are called to be channels of unity, makers of peace, and witnesses to the truth in every time and place.

canonized
A deceased Catholic's having been publicly and officially proclaimed a saint.

They do so when they speak together with one voice, especially in an Ecumenical Council.

Because of Apostolic Succession and papal infallibility, all Catholics throughout time, whether in the third century or the twenty-first, whether in Korea or Guatemala or France, share one faith that goes all the way back to Christ himself. The God who, in Jesus, promised to be with us "until the end of the age" (Matthew 28:20) has guaranteed that all of us will continue to have access to the truth until Christ comes again in glory. ♱

Article 20 The Lives of the Saints

Although God is active in the life of every person, we can especially perceive God at work in the lives of the saints, holy men and women of every time and place.

The Saints as Models of Holiness

Christ's Church is a Communion of Saints, a gathering of holy people. Some are living on earth, and some are living with God in Heaven. Those people whom the Church has officially **canonized** as saints have led lives of exemplary holiness. However, the saints are not superheroes; they are simply ordinary people who lived in the midst of difficulties, uncertainty, and suffering. Despite these circumstances they made extraordinary choices to put their faith into action. Their lives can teach us to do the same.

If you read about the lives of the saints, you may be amazed by their courage, patience, and wisdom. Many of the saints were misunderstood during their own lifetimes, their holiness being recognized only much later. For example,

Pray It!

Prayer for Unity

Lord, you desire truth deep down within us: in the secret of our hearts, you teach us wisdom. Teach us to encourage one another along the road to unity. Show us the conversion necessary for reconciliation. Give to each of us a new, truly ecumenical heart, we pray you. Amen.

the family of Saint Thomas Aquinas didn't approve of his decision to become a priest. They even kidnapped him to try to get him to change his mind! The father of Saint Francis of Assisi was similarly perplexed when his son announced his decision to renounce the family's business in favor of a simple life of preaching and begging. Saint Katharine Drexel, a nineteenth-century heiress from Philadelphia, used her inheritance to found schools for African Americans and Native Americans. Her friends and family members thought she was wasting her money—and her time. In these and other trying situations, the saints persevered in holiness. They stayed faithful to the God who called them to take great risks for the sake of the Gospel.

The Saints as Intercessors

Have you ever asked a good friend to pray for you when you were facing a difficult situation? The saints are not physically present on earth—they are living with God in Heaven—yet we can ask them to pray for us too. Regarding all those who have gone before us, especially the saints, the *Catechism* states: "Their intercession is their most exalted service to God's plan. We can and should ask them to intercede for us and for the whole world" (2683).

Saint Francis is the patron saint of animals, families, and the environment. Saint Clare is the patron saint of healthy eyes, television, and telephones. Research the patron saints for activities you like to do or causes that are important to you.

© Alinari/Art Resource, NY

Many saints are traditionally considered to be the patrons of specific issues or causes. Have you ever prayed that Saint Anthony of Padua would help you to find something you lost? Then you know he is the patron of lost items. You may also know that Saint Jude is the patron of desperate situations and Saint Valentine of lovers. But did you also know that Saint Martha is the patron of waiters and waitresses? or that Saint Clare is the patron of television? There is even a patron saint of the Internet—Saint Isidore of Seville.

Catholics do not worship the saints. Only God is worthy of worship and adoration, and only God can answer our prayers. When we pray to the saints, we ask them to pray with us and for us, just as we ask faith-filled friends on earth to offer prayers on our behalf.

The Saints as Companions

Knowing stories of the saints can be like having an extended family—people we can turn to for advice, look to for inspiration, and ask to accompany us as we face new challenges each day. Saint Gregory of Nyssa once said that the true goal of a Christian life is to become God's friend. The saints have truly been God's friends through the centuries. By their witness they invite us to be God's friends too—faithful, loyal, and true. ✝

Live It!

Becoming Friends of God

The Church reminds us that we are all called to holiness—that is, to be saintly people. But how can you do this in your everyday, ordinary life? One way is by becoming a good friend of God. You can get to know him better through daily spiritual practices such as the Eucharist, prayer, and Scripture reading. You can learn to do your studies and other activities with and for him. You can help others to become friends of his by your example and word. You can try, as Jesus showed us, to do what pleases God in everything.

Part Review

1. What is significant about Christianity's being rooted in Judaism?

2. Explain how the Gospels developed.

3. What criteria did the early Church Fathers use to determine which books formed the canon of the New Testament?

4. Name the two primary ways the Church passes on Revelation and explain how these ways are related.

5. Explain the difference between Tradition with a capital *T* and tradition with a small *t*.

6. How do we know that the beliefs and teachings of the Church really come from God?

7. What is the attitude of the Church toward other religions?

8. What can we learn from the lives of the saints? How can they help us?

Part 3

Discovering God in Creation

Do you have favorite authors or film directors? You probably don't know them personally, but you may know something about them because of the themes, characters, and settings of their books and films.

We can know something of God in the same way. "Ever since the creation of the world, [God's] invisible attributes of eternal power and divinity have been able to be understood and perceived in what he has made" (Romans 1:20). In these words Saint Paul shares with us a powerful truth. Our God is invisible, but we need look no further than creation to glimpse his goodness, power, and glory. "Creation" includes many things—our daily experiences, the people with whom we share our lives, the natural world, and our own intellectual abilities. Because we believe that God is the Source of all that is, there is nothing that *cannot* speak to us of his wisdom and love. Exploring the many ways we can encounter God helps us to grow in our awareness of his faithful presence, trusting that nothing—and no one—is outside the realm of God's care.

The topics covered is this part are:

- Article 21: "Discovering God in Our Daily Lives" (page 73)

- Article 22: "Discovering God in the Faith of Others" (page 76)

- Article 23: "Discovering God in the Natural World" (page 79)

- Article 24: "Discovering God through the Human Intellect" (page 81)

Article 21 Discovering God in Our Daily Lives

We can discover God's goodness and glory not only in the Scriptures and Tradition but also in the events and experiences of our everyday lives. In fact, our Divine Father wants to be known by us. For this reason the Holy Spirit reaches out to us, transforming our daily experiences into powerful encounters with God's wisdom and love.

"Find God in All Things"

Saint Ignatius of Loyola was the sixteenth-century Spanish priest who founded the Jesuits. He told those who sought his spiritual counsel to "find God in all things." He meant that every experience of our lives can make us aware of God's presence if we devote time and energy to reflecting on our experiences. God is not confined to certain places, like church buildings, or to certain times, like when we close our eyes to pray; rather, Saint Ignatius tells us, God infuses *all* places and *all* times.

There is no experience—good or bad—that cannot teach us and lead us into closer communion with God. For example, from the pain of suffering, we can learn compassion. From the struggle of making a difficult decision, we can learn wisdom. From the joy of success, we can learn gratitude. Through all the events of our lives, he works on us like a potter works on clay, shaping and molding us into the people we were created to be. God says through the prophet Jeremiah, "Indeed, like clay in the hand of the potter, so are you in my hand" (Jeremiah 18:6).

Catholic Wisdom

Jesuit Order and Education

The Jesuit order is also known for its commitment to education. In the United States alone, twenty-eight colleges and universities are a part of the Jesuit educational tradition. These include Loyola University New Orleans, Boston College, Gonzaga University, Saint Louis University, and Xavier University.

The Practice of Prayer

Even if we believe God is active in our lives, in order to be actively aware of this presence, we must commit ourselves to frequent prayer, asking the Holy Spirit to teach and guide us. Saint Ignatius recommended that his followers conduct an *examen* at the end of each day. It would serve as a way of increasing their awareness of God's presence. An *examen* can take many forms, but the basic steps are the following:

- quieting ourselves, asking God to enlighten and guide our minds and hearts
- reviewing the experiences of our day, noticing how we responded to and interacted with people (When did we act with love? When did we act with selfishness?)
- asking for God's forgiveness for the times in the day when we sinned
- offering gratitude for the blessings of the day
- seeking strength for all we will face the next day

Try to engage regularly in this practice of the *examen* or a similar form of daily prayer. You will see more with eyes of faith. You will notice God's grace, love, and wisdom offered to you in the midst of a conversation, a class, a game, or a quiet moment. You will realize, with the great Jesuit poet Gerard Manley Hopkins, that "the world is charged with the grandeur of God." ✝

Saint Ignatius encouraged his followers to do a daily *examen* as part of their prayer life. For the next several days, set aside time each night to pray and do an *examen,* following the steps above.

© Bill Wittman/www.wpwittman.com

Venerable Catherine McAuley of Dublin

When we become more aware of the Revelation of God in our everyday experiences, amazing things can happen.

Catherine McAuley was born in Dublin, Ireland, in 1778. She was a Catholic in a country largely controlled by Protestants. Her father, who died when Catherine was only five, was known for his generous service to the poor, offering beggars food and shelter in the family home. Catherine's mother died fifteen years later, and Catherine was sent to live with various friends and relatives. Finally, she settled with the Callaghans, a couple who had no children of their own. As she grew into adulthood, Catherine never forgot her father's example. She noticed those who were suffering in Dublin. She observed the plight of the poor and the sick, especially women and children.

When the Callaghans died, Catherine got a big surprise. They left all their money—well over a million dollars by today's standards—to her. She now had the means to become a wealthy socialite, and she even received several marriage proposals. But she politely refused each one. She had never forgotten the suffering poor of Dublin. Now she was finally in a position to relieve their burdens. She bought property and built House of Mercy, a school for the poor and a shelter for servant girls fleeing abusive situations. In time Catherine and her first coworkers took religious vows and became the first Sisters of Mercy. This religious order continues to serve the poor—especially women and children—throughout the world.

The Holy Spirit spoke to Catherine McAuley in the events and experiences of her life, even when she was quite young. Her faithful listening changed the course of her life and was a great gift to the Church and world. What amazing things will result from your faithful listening to God?

Design by Judy Ward, RSM, from the original painting by Cloy Kent. Used with permission from Mercy Iowa City.

cloistered

Adjective indicating a religious order whose members rarely leave the monastery or convent that is their home.

Article 22 Discovering God in the Faith of Others

We are never alone as we seek to live in fidelity to the truth that the Divine Father has revealed through his Son, Jesus. Thanks to the Holy Spirit, the faith of other believers is a powerful witness and support for us. We can look to both those who have gone before us and those with whom we share our lives today.

The Example of the Early Church

When Jesus sent out his followers to preach and heal in his name, he never asked them to go it alone. Instead he sent them in pairs so they could help and encourage each other. For example, the Gospel of Luke describes one of these times: Jesus "appointed seventy-[two] others whom he sent ahead of him in pairs to every town and place he intended to visit" (10:1). After Jesus' death and Resurrection, his disciples continued to follow his example by creating communities of faith. The Acts of the Apostles describes how the early Christians drew strength from their life in community:

> They devoted themselves to the teaching of the apostles and to the communal life, to the breaking of the bread and to the prayers. . . . Every day they devoted themselves to meeting together in the temple area and to breaking bread in their homes. They ate their meals with exultation and sincerity of heart, praising God and enjoying favor with all the people. (2:42,46–47)

Although these early Christians were not walking an easy road—they would be ridiculed, misunderstood, and persecuted—their shared life of faith enabled them to persevere in holiness.

The Importance of Family

Among those people who sustain our lives of faith by revealing God to us, our family is of foundational importance. The *Catechism* refers to the family as a "domestic church." It states that "believing families are of primary importance as centers of living, radiant faith" (1656). Indeed, family is where we first learn about our faith. It is truly "the first school of Christian life" (1657). As we mature, our family members can encourage our growth in faith and stand by us during times of doubt and confusion. Family is truly one of God's gracious gifts to us.

Who Stirs Up Faith in You?

In the towering redwood forests of northern California, ten religious women live as a community of cloistered nuns. **Cloistered** means they rarely leave the monastery that is their home. Within its walls they live a simple life structured around six times of daily prayer. Although they engage in some work to support themselves through the sale of handcrafted items, their full-time job really is praying for the needs of the world.

Many guests visit the monastery for weekend or weeklong retreats. These visits offer chances for silence, prayer, and spiritual renewal. The visitors often find themselves deeply moved by the witness these nuns offer. The nuns' lives exemplify their faith, their humility, and the deep joy that comes from living in constant awareness of God's boundless grace.

The faith of other believers is intended by God to be a gift to us. We must then intentionally seek out those whose religious commitment is truly inspiring. Can you think of a person or group whose example spurs you to greater holiness?

© Bill Wittman/www.wpwittman.com

Communal Prayer

Remember, we are never alone in our search for God. What if family or friends let us down? We still have the whole Communion of Saints—that is, the whole community of the faithful in Heaven and on earth—with whom to share both our joys and our struggles. Indeed, Catholicism is fundamentally communal, not individualistic. This is especially clear in our lives of prayer. Though private prayer is meaningful and important, communal prayer—especially Eucharistic liturgy—is central to our Catholic identity. Celebrating the Eucharist tells us that we are together the Body of Christ. We are united by our Baptism, strengthened by the presence of Jesus in his precious Body and Blood, and sent out to be life and light for the world. What a tremendous gift to be part of this worldwide community of believers. ✝

Prayer is not always a silent and solemn act. Retreats, diocesan and national youth gatherings, and World Youth Days are opportunities for young people to gather and share in joyful praise and song.

© Bill Wittman/www.wpwittman.com

Pray It!

The Communion of Saints in the Eucharist

When we gather for Mass, we join our prayers with those of others gathered and with the Communion of Saints. The next time you attend Mass, pay special attention to the Eucharistic Prayer. You will notice that we pray for a wide range of people. We pray for the entire Church, the Pope and our local bishop, and all of the bishops and clergy, as well as all of those who have died.

When you are at Mass, really focus on praying for all the groups mentioned in the Eucharistic Prayer. You can also call to mind family and friends whom you want to include privately in these general prayers. In this way you join your prayer with the prayer of the whole Church.

Article 23 Discovering God in the Natural World

Have you ever found peace while sitting on the beach at sunset, awe while hiking through a lush forest, or amazement while flying over snow-capped mountains? Then you have come to know God in the natural world. Even small things—a plant growing on a window ledge, a flower pushing through a crack in the pavement, a dog wagging its tail—can reveal the beauty and wonder of nature and can move us to prayer and praise.

God, Creator of the Natural World

Think about it: How could something as immense as the universe, as astounding as a volcano, or as complex as a human person come from anything but a divine source? Nature tells us that God is the origin and Creator of all that is. Listening to the "message of creation" reveals to us that God is "the cause and the end of everything" (*CCC*, 46).

God did not *have* to create the world; rather, in great wisdom and love, God freely chose to bring the universe into being. As Psalm 104 states:

> How varied are your works, Lord!
>> In wisdom you have wrought them all;
>> the earth is full of your creatures.
>>>> (Verse 24)

Moreover, all creatures of the earth, because of their divine origin, reflect God's glory. Elephants and dolphins, roses and redwood trees, mushrooms and moss, planets and stars and human beings: we all share in God's "truth, goodness, and beauty" (*CCC*, 319).

The Role of Science

Belief in the divine origin of the universe does not mean that Catholics are against scientific inquiry. The *Catechism* states that there can be no real discrepancy between faith and reason; both are gifts to us from God (see 159). Addressing the topic of science in particular, the *Catechism* quotes the Vatican II document *Pastoral Constitution on the Church in* the *Modern World* (*Gaudium et Spes,* 1965): "The humble and persevering investigator of the secrets of nature is being led, as it were, by the hand of God . . . for it is God, the conserver of all things, who made them what they are"[7] (*CCC,* 159). In other words, *that* God brought the universe into being is a key religious truth, but science can inform us as to *how* this may have been accomplished. In helping us to explore the many wonders of the universe, science can also reveal God's glory to us in new and amazing ways. It can move us to awe and reverence at the work of our Creator.

Stewardship of Creation

God has graciously given us the natural world as a precious gift, and has entrusted us with stewardship of creation, a responsibility to care for and protect all the good he has created. Stewardship is a sacred obligation. God has entrusted us with this beautiful and wondrous world that sustains us in life, so we must not abuse, destroy, or harm it in any way. Rather, we must safeguard its resources and use them for the good of all people.

We need to truly fall in love with nature, allowing its beauty to touch our hearts and stir us to action. Then stew-

We each share in the responsibility to care for God's creation. What actions can you and your family take to help nurture and care for the environment?

ardship can bring us satisfaction, joy, and a renewed sense of
our own place in this vast universe. In the words of Psalm 8:

theology
Literally, "the study of
God"; the academic
discipline and effort
to understand, inter-
pret, and order our
experience of God and
Christian faith.

> When I see your heavens, the work of your fingers,
> the moon and stars that you set in place—
>
> . . . .
>
> All sheep and oxen,
> even the beasts of the field,
> The birds of the air, the fish of the sea,
> and whatever swims the paths of the seas.
> O Lord, our Lord,
> how awesome is your name through all the earth!
>
> (Verses 4,8–10) ✝

Article 24 Discovering God through the Human Intellect

A voice booming from out of a cloud. The heavens parting.
Visions of angels and other heavenly beings. Sometimes we
might imagine that we can know God with certainty only
in dramatic, literally earth-shaking, events. Though the
Scriptures do recount stories of people who experienced
God's Revelation of himself in this way, we don't need visions
to know something about God. We need look no further
than our human reason and intellect, for "the one true God,
our Creator and Lord, can be known with certainty from
his works, by the natural light of human reason" (cf. Vatican
Council I, can. 2 § 1: Denzinger-Schonmetzer, *Enchiridion
Symbolorum, definitionum et declarationum de rebus fidei et
morum* [1965] 3026) (*CCC*, 47).

The Gift of Human Intellect

The Church has a long tradition of urging us to use our
minds to grow in understanding our faith. In fact, Saint
Anselm's classic definition of **theology** is "faith seeking understanding." Saint Anselm understood that God has given us
the gift of the intellectual capacity to understand faith more
fully. We can use this gift to study the Scriptures, read the
lives of the saints, learn the history of Church teachings, and
engage in other intellectual efforts related to the faith. Taking
responsibility to do such things is part of what it means to be

© Falconia/shutterstock.com

Our intellect and our ability to reason are two of the greatest gifts God has given us.

a mature Catholic. Through these efforts we use the gifts of reason, logic, and intellect that our Creator gave us to know and love him more deeply.

How Can We Speak about God?

Although we can know something of God through our human reason and intellect, the language we use to express that knowledge can never fully capture the Divine Mystery. "Our human words always fall short of the mystery of God" (*CCC*, 42). This is why there is such a great diversity of representations of God in the Scriptures. No single image could ever fully express who God is. These images are drawn from the created world, "for from the greatness and the beauty of created things / their original author, by analogy, is seen" (Wisdom 13:5). Thus the Scriptures depict God with images of nature, such as light, rock, fire, and water. They refer to God with images of humanity, such as potter, shepherd, king, mother, and husband. Each of these ways

Live It!

Using Your Mind to Study Religion

Our minds are gifts from God, who wants us to use them well. God especially wants us to use them to learn about him and his relationship with humanity. In a real sense, studies in religion are the most important studies we can undertake. When we study our faith, we can grow closer to God.

Here are some pointers that can help you grow closer to God and that can have a positive effect on your relationships with others:

- Try to take your religion studies seriously.
- Seek to grasp and apply the things your class reads and discusses.
- Pray about points that strike you.
- Strive to make the faith really your own.

of speaking of God gives us meaningful insight into his goodness and glory. No description of God is ever complete. We must not fall into the trap of thinking that God is literally a rock, a shepherd, a king, or anything but God. God is "the inexpressible, the incomprehensible, the invisible, the ungraspable"[8] (*CCC*, 42). ✞

Saint Thomas Aquinas

© Alinari Archives/CORBIS

Saint Thomas Aquinas was an Italian Dominican priest who lived in the thirteenth century. He is considered to be one of the greatest Catholic theologians who ever lived. His powerful intellect allowed him to gain respect as the author of many works and as a clear thinker and respected university lecturer.

Aquinas was thought to be innovative in his time. He used the writings of the pagan Greek thinker Aristotle in his own writings on theology. His *Summa Theologica* is a synthesis of major theological topics of the day. It is still considered a classic of Western thought.

Normally the Church celebrates a saint's feast day on the day of his or her death—the day when the saint was born into eternal life with God. However, Aquinas's feast day is January 28—the day his relics were transferred to their final resting place. In this the Church pays homage to the holiness of the intellectual life. In using our human reason to study and ponder the truths of our faith, we glimpse God's eternal glory while we live on earth.

Part Review

1. What did Saint Ignatius of Loyola mean when he said to seek to "find God in all things"?

2. What is the purpose of a daily *examen*? How is it done?

3. Why is communal prayer important?

4. Why is there no real disagreement between faith and science?

5. What does being stewards of creation mean?

6. How can we use God's gift of intellect to know God better?

7. Why does Sacred Scripture use such a wide variety of images to represent God?

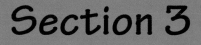

Jesus: The Definitive Revelation of God

Part 1

The Incarnation

The doctrine that the Son of God assumed a human nature to become Jesus of Nazareth is one of the distinctive marks of Christian faith. Our God took on human flesh, being conceived in Mary's womb, in order to save us from sin and death. The Incarnation truly united humanity with God, for in sharing our humanity, God allowed us to share in his divinity.

When we speak of the Incarnation, we often speak of Jesus as the Word Made Flesh (see John 1:14). This image helps us to remember that the Incarnation is the fulfillment of a long relationship God had initiated with humanity and, in particular, with the people of Israel, many centuries earlier. God made a covenant with Abraham and all his descendants. Finally, in the fullness of time, he sent his only Son to earth. God's covenant relationship with the Jews, the first people to receive, accept, and live by God's Word, is still valid even to the present day. However, because of the Incarnation, God's Word is fully, definitively, and uniquely present as Jesus Christ.

The topics covered is this part are:

Article 25 What Is the Incarnation?

The Incarnation can be defined as "the fact that the Son of God assumed a human nature in order to accomplish our salvation in it" (*Catechism of the Catholic Church [CCC]*, 461). That the Son of God actually came in the flesh to save us from sin and death is "the distinctive sign of Christian faith" (463). Let's spend some time exploring this great and miraculous mystery.

By the Power of the Holy Spirit

Luke's Gospel tells us how the Incarnation occurred through the power of the Holy Spirit. The angel Gabriel announces to Mary that she will give birth to a son named Jesus, which means "God saves." Mary responds with a question: "How can this be, since I have no relations with a man?" (1:34). Gabriel tells Mary: "The holy Spirit will come upon you, and the power of the Most High will overshadow you. Therefore the child to be born will be called holy, the Son of God" (1:35). This passage helps us to understand that Jesus was conceived by the Holy Spirit in order to begin his saving work among us. The action of the Holy Spirit in Mary gives humanity the great gift of "Emmanuel," God with us (see Matthew 1:23).

From All Eternity

Jesus' conception in Mary's womb began the *earthly* existence of the Son of God. His *heavenly* existence is eternal— that is, without a beginning or an end. The beautiful poem that begins John's Gospel states:

> In the beginning was the Word,
>   and the Word was with God,
>   and the Word was God.
> He was in the beginning with God.
>   (1:1–2)

At a certain point in history, more than two thousand years ago, the Word of God "became flesh / and made his dwelling among us" (verse 14). When the Son of God became flesh, he did not stop being God. He had always been God, but now he was a man as well. To put it another way, he had always been the Son of God, but now he was also the Son of Mary. "The Incarnation is therefore the mystery of the wonderful union of the divine and human natures in the one person of the Word" (*CCC*, 483).

Over the years various heresies, or incorrect beliefs, have denied the fullness of the Incarnation. For example, some people mistakenly think Jesus started out as a human and then somehow became God over the course of his life. Others err in thinking that Jesus was not God at all but was just a really special person God chose, at some point in his life, for a special mission. However, Jesus Christ, the Eternal Son of God and the Second Person of the Trinity, was always God—before, during, and after his life on earth. He was God "by nature and not by adoption" (*CCC*, 465). ✝

The angel Gabriel's announcement to Mary that she would give birth to Jesus is known as the Annunciation. The Feast of the Annunciation, celebrated each year on March 25, honors Mary's courageous "yes" to God.

© Bill Wittman/www.wpwittman.com

Pray It!

Ten Simple Words

In the Gospel of Luke, after the angel Gabriel shares with Mary that she will give birth to Jesus, Mary responds by saying: "Behold, I am the handmaid of the Lord. May it be done to me according to your word" (1:38). This response shows Mary's willingness to do what God is asking of her.

The next time you pray, consider simply praying, "May it be done to me according to your word." This simple prayer can change your life. If you mean what you pray, these ten simple words will open you up to all that God desires for you.

The Sacred Heart of Jesus

Have you ever thought deeply about the reality of the Incarnation? As a real human being, Jesus breathed, ate, drank, laughed, cried, smiled, and had unique facial expressions. He had a human body just like ours, with hands, feet, arms, legs, bones, arteries, lungs, and a heart. Devotion to the Sacred Heart of Jesus powerfully reminds us of the truth of the Incarnation—that the Son of God walked among us as an actual flesh-and-blood man.

Prayer to the Sacred Heart of Jesus began in the Middle Ages, but it was Saint Margaret Mary Alacoque, a Sister of the Visitation living in seventeenth-century France, who made this devotion popular. Jesus appeared to Saint Margaret Mary in visions. He told her that she had been chosen to spread devotion to his Sacred Heart, especially through celebration of the Eucharist on the first Friday of each month. Like many saints and visionaries, Alacoque's ideas were not accepted during her lifetime. In 1856, nearly two hundred years after Saint Margaret Mary's death, Pope Pius IX placed the Solemnity of the Sacred Heart on the Church's liturgical calendar. It continues to be celebrated each year on the third Friday after Pentecost. This year let this feast day remind you of the awesome gift of God's saving presence among us as one who "has loved us all with a human heart" (*CCC,* 478).

holy day of obligation

Feast day in the liturgical year on which, in addition to Sundays, Catholics are obliged to participate in the Eucharist.

Article 26 Mary's Role in the Incarnation

In order for the Incarnation to occur, the Eternal Word of God needed a human mother. This woman, prepared from all eternity for this role, was Mary of Nazareth, the Blessed Mother. Her willingness to say yes to God's gracious plan made our salvation possible. In her very body, the Holy Spirit completes all the preparations for Christ's coming. By this action of the Holy Spirit, God the Father gives the world the great gift of Emmanuel, "God with us."

Because she is the mother of Jesus Christ, the Eternal Son of God made man who is God himself, Mary is also truly the "Mother of God," which in Greek is translated as *Theotokos*. This is a title of honor the Church has bestowed on Mary. Devotion to Mary, a key feature of Catholicism, centers on her unique role in salvation history and on three important doctrines about her.

Mary's Immaculate Conception

The Solemnity of the Immaculate Conception of Mary is celebrated on December 8, a **holy day of obligation.** (Holy days of obligation are feast days on which Catholics are obliged to

Live It!

Holy Days of Obligation

The Church calendar is called the liturgical year. In the course of the liturgical year, the whole mystery of Christ unfolds, from his Incarnation and Nativity through his Ascension into Heaven, to Pentecost and our expectation of his return in glory. The Church's cycle of prayers and Scripture readings recall the important events from Christ's life and his work of salvation. We recall these events on Sundays and on the Church's holy days of obligation. Along with all the Sundays of the year, there are six holy days of obligation. On these days we are obliged to participate in the Eucharist. Make a commitment to attend Mass on these holy days:

- Christmas (December 25)
- Solemnity of the Blessed Virgin Mary, the Mother of God (January 1)
- Ascension of the Lord (forty days after Easter)
- Assumption of the Blessed Virgin Mary (August 15)
- All Saints' Day (November 1)
- Immaculate Conception of the Blessed Virgin Mary (December 8)

participate in the Eucharist, the same as on Sundays.) Many people make the mistake of thinking that we celebrate Jesus' conception on this day. In fact, the Immaculate Conception celebrates the day on which *Mary* was conceived in the womb of her mother, Saint Ann. Because Mary was to fulfill the absolutely unique role of carrying the Eternal Son of God into the world, God allowed her to be conceived without **Original Sin.** This is why her conception is described as immaculate. She was redeemed from the first moment of her life and remained free from all **personal sin** throughout her life.

Mary's Perpetual Virginity

Jesus was conceived in Mary's womb through the power of the Holy Spirit. Luke's Gospel states this clearly: "The holy Spirit will come upon you, and the power of the Most High will overshadow you" (1:35). Therefore Mary became pregnant with Jesus while remaining a virgin. Mary remained a virgin throughout her life, as a sign of her total dedication to serving God as "the handmaid of the Lord" (Luke 1:38).

Although Jesus was Mary's only biological child, Mary is a spiritual mother to all of us. The Second Vatican Council's *Dogmatic Constitution on the Church* (*Lumen Gentium*, 1964) reminds us of this fact and what it means. It states that "the Catholic Church, taught by the Holy Spirit, honors her [Mary] with filial affection and piety as a most beloved mother" (53). As any attentive mother, Mary can pray with us and for us. She acts as our advocate, comforter, companion, and friend.

Several passages in the New Testament refer to Jesus' brothers and sisters (see, for example, Mark 3:32 and Galatians 1:19).

Original Sin
The sin by which the first humans disobeyed God and thereby lost their original holiness and became subject to death. Original Sin is transmitted to every person born into the world, except Mary and Jesus.

personal sin
Any deliberate offense, in thought, word, or deed, against the will of God.

One of the many titles Mary has that reflects her special place in the life of Jesus and the Church is Queen of Heaven. What other titles for Mary are you familiar with?

Given that Mary remained a virgin her whole life, what are we to make of these passages? There are several possible explanations. The *Catechism* states that "the Church has always understood these passages as not referring to other children of the Virgin Mary" (500). These individuals are "close relations of Jesus, according to an Old Testament expression"[1] (500). Eastern Catholics and Orthodox Christians have traditionally believed that Joseph was a widower when he married Mary and that the people referred to as Jesus' siblings are in fact Joseph's children from his former marriage. Both explanations help us to understand these Scripture passages in light of the Church's firm and constant teaching on Mary's perpetual virginity.

Mary's Assumption

Mary had the great honor and blessing of carrying the physical presence of the Eternal Son of God into the world in her own body. Therefore, when she died, God did not allow her body to decay. God brought her whole being—body and soul—into Heaven. Roman Catholics celebrate this event as

There are countless images of Mary, both classical and contemporary. What do you think the artist of this stained-glass piece was trying to communicate about Mary?

the Solemnity of the Assumption. This is another holy day of obligation. Eastern Catholics and Orthodox Christians call it Mary's Dormition (or "falling asleep"). Both groups celebrate this special end to Mary's earthly life on August 15. ✝

27 Jesus: The Word Made Flesh

Article

The Gospel of John tells us:

> And the Word became flesh
> and made his dwelling among us,
> and we saw his glory,
> the glory as of the Father's only Son,
> full of grace and truth.
>
> (1:14)

This "Word" (in Greek, *Logos*) is the Eternal Son of God. The Word is with God the Father in Heaven for all eternity, along with the Holy Spirit. At a particular point in history, the Word became incarnate (flesh) in Mary's womb.

God Prepared Humanity for the Incarnation

The Old Testament tells the history of God's self-revelation to humanity. It shows how God guides, corrects, challenges, and comforts us after sin had damaged our original friendship with God. God spoke to Abraham, telling him to leave his home and journey with his wife, Sarah, to a new land as the ancestors of the Chosen People (see Genesis 12:1). God gave the ancient Israelites the Law at Mount Sinai. He made clear his desires and expectations (see Exodus, chapter 20).

God sent the prophets, placing in their mouths and on their hearts the very word he wished them to speak. They called the Israelites back to fidelity to the Covenant (see, for example, Jeremiah 1:4). Through these many centuries, God drew closer and closer to the people, until, in the fullness of time, "God sent his Son, born of a woman, born under the law, to ransom those under the law, so that we might receive adoption" (Galatians 4:4–5). Thus, throughout the history of the ancient Israelites, God prepared humanity for the ultimate self-revelation, the Incarnation of the Word—the coming of his Son—and for the development of the Church.

Fulfillment, Not Replacement

In the Gospel of Matthew, Jesus says to his disciples: "Do not think that I have come to abolish the law or the prophets. I have come not to abolish but to fulfill. Amen, I say to you, until heaven and earth pass away, not the smallest letter or the smallest part of a letter will pass from the law" (5:17–18). This passage helps us to understand that Jesus fulfills, but does not replace, God's Law, given to the ancient Israelites. *Fulfills* means that Jesus perfects the law, reveals its ultimate meaning, and redeems any sins people had committed against it. We know that Jesus does not replace the Law, because God's Covenant with the Israelites, today known as Jews, is still active and valid. God's fidelity to the people he has chosen endures forever. The Vatican II document *Declaration on the Relation of the Church to Non-Christian Religions* (*Nostra Aetate*, 1965) states: "God holds the Jews most dear for the sake of their Fathers; He does not repent of the gifts He makes or of the calls He issues" (4).

These are just some examples of how the Old Testament prepares us for the coming of Christ, whose saving work and mission are clearly revealed in the New Testament. Both Testaments reveal that the Divine Word of God is fully present in a unique, definitive way in the Person of Jesus Christ. ✝

Catholic Wisdom

Alpha and Omega

Jesus is sometimes referred to as the Alpha and Omega. Alpha and omega are the first and last letters of the Greek alphabet. Together they signify the eternal presence of Jesus Christ. The celebrant says these words as he prepares the Easter candle at the Easter Vigil: "Christ yesterday and today / the Beginning and the End / the Alpha / and the Omega / All time belongs to him / and all the ages / To him be glory and power / through every age and for ever. Amen" (*Roman Missal*).

Mary, Seat of Wisdom

The Church's titles for Mary are rooted in what the Church believes about Christ (see CCC, 487). For example, because Jesus is the Word Made Flesh, we have the beautiful image of Mary as the Seat of Wisdom.

In the Old Testament, Wisdom is personified as a woman who invites all people to share in her life and to dine at her table. For example, in the Book of Sirach:

> Wisdom sings her own praises,
>> before her own people she proclaims her glory;
> In the assembly of the Most High she opens her mouth,
>> in the presence of his hosts she declares her worth:
>
> . . . .
>
> "Come to me, all you that yearn for me,
>> and be filled with my fruits;
> You will remember me as sweeter than honey,
>> better to have than the honeycomb."
>
> (24:1–2,18–19)

Because the Old Testament figure of Wisdom is female, the Catholic Church "has often read the most beautiful texts on wisdom in relation to Mary"[2] (CCC, 721). This, along with our belief that God's Word, made flesh in Mary's womb, is full of wisdom for us, has given Mary the title Seat of Wisdom.

Images of Mary as the Seat of Wisdom usually show her seated on a throne, with the child Jesus on her lap. In some images Jesus holds the Book of the Gospels. This means that the Word Made Flesh is offering the very gift of Wisdom to the viewer.

collects

Prayers offered by the person leading an assembly in communal prayer.

Article 28 The Union of God with Humanity

The Incarnation brought humanity and God closer together than we would ever otherwise be able to be. Because of the Incarnation, we are able to see God's human face, to renew our relationship with God, and even to share in the divine nature.

Jesus, the Revealer and Mediator

The Incarnation was an absolutely singular, unique event. Never before (and never since!) had God assumed human nature. Therefore Jesus, as God Made Flesh, fulfills two unique roles.

First, Jesus reveals God the Father to us. In John's Gospel, Jesus states: "Whoever has seen me has seen the Father" (14:9). Because he is the Divine Son of the Father, Jesus is truly the human face of God among us. Are there times when you wonder what God would do, say, or think? You simply need to look to the actions, words, and thoughts of Jesus, as recorded in the New Testament and as interpreted by the Church through the centuries.

Second, Jesus is the one and only mediator between humanity and God. He is like a bridge that connects earth with Heaven, making God accessible to us even though we had lost God's friendship through sin. The Incarnation and all the subsequent events of Jesus' life, especially his death and Resurrection, give us a new and certain path to God and to salvation.

Sharing in the Divine Life

Because Jesus shared in our lives, we are able to share in God's life. Saint Paul's Letter to the Colossians states, "For in [Jesus] dwells the whole fullness of the deity bodily, and you share in this fullness in him, who is the head of every principality and power" (2:9–10). The Second Letter of Peter makes the same point, saying, "He has bestowed on us the precious and very great promises, so that through them you may come to share in the divine nature" (1:4).

Sharing in the divine life of God means we are drawn into communion with the Trinity. During our time on earth,

The Christmas Liturgy: Celebrating the Incarnation

Does your family attend Christmas Mass together, either at midnight or on Christmas morning? If so, you may have been too excited and distracted to really listen to the prayers of the liturgy when you were a small child. Now you can appreciate more deeply the beauty of what we celebrate on Christmas Day. (Officially this is known as the Solemnity of the Nativity of the Lord.)

The prayers of the Christmas liturgy reflect core truths about the Incarnation in moving and poetic language. Consider these brief excerpts from the **collects** and other prayers of the liturgies of Christmas, quoted from the *Roman Missal*:

- "grant, we pray, that we, who have known the mysteries of his light on earth, / may also delight in his gladness in heaven."
- "May [we] be found in the likeness of Christ, / in whom our nature is united to you."
- "may we serve you all the more eagerly / for knowing that in [the coming festivities] / you make manifest the beginnings of our redemption."
- "we pray, / that we may share in the divinity of Christ, / who humbled himself to share in our humanity."

Next Christmas remind yourself to pay close attention to the meaningful and striking language of the prayers of the liturgy. Praying with these words, even now, can deepen our appreciation for the great gift of the Incarnation.

© iStockphoto.com/Lisa Thornberg

Beatific Vision
Direct encounter and sight of God in the glory of Heaven.

we are profoundly united with God through our Baptism, through our sharing in the Eucharistic feast, and through our participation in the other Sacraments of the Church. We are invited to cooperate with God's plan for our lives and to participate actively in our salvation. During our life after death, we will experience the **Beatific Vision,** enjoying God's presence and glory forever.

Many of the early Church Fathers were truly awed by the gift God gave us in the Incarnation. In their writings they pondered with amazement the beautiful idea of God's inviting us to share in the divine nature. Saint Athanasius's famous line is often quoted in this regard: "The Son of God became man so that we might become God"[3] (*CCC*, 460). A version of this idea has even found its way into our liturgy. The next time you are at Mass, listen closely to the prayers the priest offers as he prepares our gifts of bread and wine. Sometimes these words are not audible, but you may hear the priest pray these words: "By the mystery of this water and wine, may we come to share in the divinity of Christ, who humbled himself to share in our humanity" *(Roman Missal).* ☦

Part Review

1. What is the Incarnation?

2. What is the significance of the Incarnation for us?

3. What is Mary's role in the Incarnation?

4. Define *Theotokos* and explain the significance of this term.

5. Jesus comes to fulfill, not to replace, the Law God gave to the Israelites. What does this mean?

6. Describe two unique roles that Jesus, as God Made Flesh, fulfills.

7. What does it mean that we are able to share in the divine life of God?

Part 2

The Two Natures of Jesus: Human and Divine

The Scriptures and Tradition teach that Jesus Christ is true God and true man. Exploring various aspects of Jesus' life will equip us to understand more completely how God and humanity came together in an absolutely unique way in Jesus of Nazareth.

Key features of Jesus' life that are worthy of our study and investigation include his friendships, his emotions, and his religious life as a faithful Jew. These features remind us that Jesus lived a fully human life, complete with both joys and challenges. It is also crucial to grasp that Jesus lived, taught, and ministered in the political and cultural world of the Roman Empire. The meaning of many of his teachings becomes clearer when considered against this backdrop.

Learning as much as we can about Jesus' earthly life enriches our appreciation of the Incarnation. It sheds light on the many titles devout Christians, through the centuries, have applied to the One who lived and died on earth in order to save us.

The topics covered is this part are:

^{Article}
29 Jesus: A Human Mind, a Human Heart

The doctrine of the Incarnation affirms that Jesus was a real man. He was not someone who simply looked like one or who was pretending to be one. As the Vatican II document *Pastoral Constitution on the Church in the Modern World* (*Gaudium et Spes,* 1965) states: "He worked with human hands, he thought with a human mind. He acted with a human will, and with a human heart he loved" (22). Jesus was truly like us in all things except sin.

sanctifies
Makes holy; sanctification is the process of becoming closer to God and growing in holiness.

The Joys and Trials of Human Nature

Jesus experienced both the blessings and the difficulties of normal life, just as we do. Jesus had close friends and family members with whom he developed genuine relationships. The Gospels tell us that he shared meals and celebrations with those people. He attended the wedding feast at Cana (see John 2:1–11). He had dinner at the home of Martha, Mary, and Lazarus (see Luke 10:38–42). Jesus also enjoyed visiting the homes of those who were misunderstood or outcast by society, such as Simon the Pharisee (see Luke 7:36–50) and Zacchaeus the tax collector (see Luke 19:1–10). Like us, Jesus delighted in the spirit of friendship that results when people gather around a table to share a meal.

Jesus also experienced frustration, hunger, pain, fatigue, suffering, and sorrow. He knew all the circumstances that can make life hard. For example, following his forty days of fasting in the desert, Jesus is weakened by hunger and thirst, making him a target of temptation by the Devil (see Matthew 4:1–11). Later in his life, Jesus cries when he hears that his dear friend Lazarus has died (see John 11:35). Most obviously, in his Passion and death, Jesus feels genuine pain—psychological fear and emotional anxiety in the garden at Gethsemane and physical torment on the cross.

Jesus' fully human life—with all its joys and struggles—**sanctifies** every part of our own lives. Because of the Incarnation, the blessings of our lives—like friends, family, and the beauty of nature—are signs of God's presence. In addition, our struggles, trials, and difficulties are a way for us to grow in trusting and loving God. Our faith in the Incarnation enables us to embrace every good day and every bad day of our earthly lives as a unique opportunity to grow in holiness.

Jesus Never Stops Being God

In exploring the mystery of Jesus the man, we must not forget that at no point does Jesus cease to be God—not in his birth, life, emotions, friendships, or death. Even as he

Martha, Mary, and Lazarus: Faithful Friends of the Lord

Martha, Mary, and Lazarus are three siblings who live together in Bethany, a town not far from Jerusalem. In the Gospels Jesus often visits the home of these dear friends.

Martha shows great hospitality toward Jesus as a guest in her home (see Luke 10:38–42). She confesses her faith in him as "the Messiah, the Son of God, the one who is coming into the world" (John 11:27).

Mary faithfully absorbs Jesus' words, sitting at his feet in the traditional posture of a disciple listening to her teacher (see Luke 10:38–42). Later, as Jesus prepares for death, she anoints his feet with perfumed oil and dries them with her hair (see John 12:1–8).

Lazarus is silent in these stories, but Jesus' raising him to life after he has been dead four days is one of the most dramatic miracles in all of the New Testament (see John 11:1–44).

Martha, Mary, and Lazarus allow Jesus to experience one of life's greatest joys: friendship. Friends are truly God's gift to us. It seems that Jesus himself knew that "a faithful friend is a sturdy shelter . . . is beyond price . . . is a life-saving remedy" (Sirach 6:14–16).

Jesus' human heart felt joy, happiness, temptation, and pain. This picture depicts Jesus' being tempted by the Devil after forty days of fasting. How does it help you to know that Jesus also experienced temptation?

© Brooklyn Museum/Corbis

lives on earth, Jesus remains at all times the Son of God, the Second Person of the Trinity. As the *Catechism* states, "In his soul as in his body, Christ thus expresses humanly the divine ways of the Trinity"[4] (470). ✝

Article

30 Jesus: A Faithful Jew

We cannot comprehend Jesus' earthly life without focusing our attention on his religious identity as a faithful Jew. Jesus' "religious life was that of a Jew obedient to the law of God"[5] (*CCC*, 531).

Raised in a Jewish Home

The very earliest stories of Jesus' infancy make clear that Mary and Joseph bring him up in accord with Jewish laws and traditions. For example, Jesus is circumcised on the eighth day after his birth (see Luke 2:21). From the time of Abraham and Sarah, **circumcision** has been the physical sign of God's Covenant with the people of Israel. The *Catechism* describes the circumcision of Jesus as "the sign of his incorporation into Abraham's descendants, into the people of the

circumcision

The act, required by Jewish law, of removing the foreskin of the penis. Since the time of Abraham, it has been a sign of God's Covenant relationship with the Jewish people.

scribes
Jewish government officials and scholars of the Law.

Pharisees
A Jewish sect at the time of Jesus known for its strict adherence to the Law.

Sadducees
A Jewish sect at the time of Jesus known for its strong commitment to the Temple in Jerusalem.

anti-Semitism
Prejudice against the Jewish people.

covenant. It is the sign of his submission to the Law[6] and his deputation to Israel's worship, in which he will participate throughout his life" (527).

Later, Mary and Joseph bring Jesus to Jerusalem to present him at the Temple (see Luke 2:22–38). In this action they follow the law of Exodus: "Consecrate to me every first-born that opens the womb among the Israelites, both of man and beast, for it belongs to me" (13:2). They also follow the law of Leviticus, which required the sacrifice of a lamb and a turtledove forty days after the birth of a baby boy (see 12:6–8). Interestingly, Mary and Joseph adhere to a variation on the law for poor families by bringing a second turtledove instead of a lamb.

Practicing His Faith

In the Gospels, Jesus celebrates Jewish holidays, such as the Feast of the Passover (see John 2:13); the Feast of Tabernacles, or Sukkoth (see John 7:2); and the Feast of the Dedication, or Hanukkah (see John 10:22). Jesus often travels to Jerusalem to mark these occasions.

Jesus also frequently demonstrates his knowledge of the Hebrew Scriptures (Old Testament). For example, look at what happens when he is tempted by the Devil (see Luke 4:1–13). He uses direct quotations from the Book of Deuteronomy to refute every point the Devil makes. Another time he is talking with a group of **scribes** and **Pharisees.** He refers to the Hebrew stories of Jonah the prophet and Solomon the king (see Matthew 12:38–42). In order to teach the **Sadducees** about resurrection, he draws on the story of Moses and the burning bush (see Mark 12:18–27). Clearly Jesus is very familiar with the

Catholic Wisdom

A Special Kind of Remembering

When Jews celebrate the Passover, they recall God's freeing the Israelites from slavery in Egypt. They don't believe, however, that the Exodus is only a past event. They believe that God is doing the same thing in the present. In a similar way, when Catholics celebrate the Eucharist, we recall what Jesus did in his life, death, and Resurrection. We celebrate that his saving action is present today. This special kind of remembering is known as anamnesis.

Scriptures of his people, for he has immersed himself in these ancient texts in his prayer and study.

One Gospel story that allows us a vivid glimpse into Jesus' religious life as a Jew occurs in Luke 4:16–22. In this passage Jesus engages in the customary practices of the Jewish people by going to the synagogue on the Sabbath. (A synagogue is a Jewish place of worship; the Sabbath is the Jewish day of prayer and rest.) There Jesus reads from the scroll of the prophet Isaiah—one of the books of the Hebrew Scriptures—and teaches the people. Together with many other Gospel stories, this passage offers us a compelling portrait of Jesus, a faithful Jew. ✝

Sr. Rose Thering

Sr. Rose Thering was a Dominican sister and university professor who devoted her life to promoting understanding between Jews and Christians. During her doctoral studies at Saint Louis University in the late 1950s, she researched the history of **anti-Semitism** in Catholic publications and sermons. When the Second Vatican Council opened in 1962, Cardinal Augustin Bea used Thering's findings to draft portions of *Nostra Aetate*, Vatican II's *Declaration on the Relation of the Church to Non-Christian Religions* (1965).

Prior to Vatican II, some Catholics had charged all Jews with the crime of deicide. They blamed the Jews of Jesus' lifetime and those of the present day for killing God. *Relation of the Church to Non-Christian Religions* condemned this belief. "Even though the Jewish authorities and those who followed their lead pressed for the death of Christ (see John 19:6), neither all Jews indiscriminately at that time, nor Jews today, can be charged with the crimes committed during his passion" (4).

Sister Rose died in 2006 at the age of eighty-five, her faith-filled and critical scholarship having left a lasting mark on Catholic theology and on Jewish-Christian relations.

Article 31 Jesus' Life in First-Century Palestine

Knowing a little bit about the historical world Jesus lived in can enrich our understanding of his life on earth. It can also help us to better understand many of his teachings.

Historical Background

Jesus lived in Palestine, which was the name the Greeks had given to the land of Israel. In fact, the influence of Greek culture was still felt in the time of Jesus, even though the Roman occupation of Palestine had begun in 63 BC. By Jesus' lifetime (approximately 4 BC–AD 30), Rome controlled the whole Mediterranean basin, from modern-day France and Spain in the west, to the Black Sea and the Caspian Sea in the northeast, to northern Africa in the south. At the time of Jesus' birth, the Roman emperor allowed local kings to rule regions in his stead, provided the local kings remained loyal to the Roman Empire. At the time of Jesus' birth, this king in Palestine was Herod. He was known as Herod the Great because of his political skills, although his reputation for cruelty and violence was formidable. You might remember the story known as "Massacre of the Innocents," in which Herod killed all the baby boys in the area because he had heard about the birth of a new king of the Jews: Jesus (see Matthew 2:16–18).

After Herod's death in 4 BC, his three sons were each given a section of Palestine to rule. One of the sons, Herod Antipas (sometimes just called Antipas to avoid confusing him with his father), ruled Galilee, the region where Jesus' hometown of Nazareth is located. Philip ruled the northeastern part of Palestine. Archelaeus ruled Judea, Samaria, and Idumea, regions of Palestine in which many events in Jesus' life occurred. However, Archelaeus was such an unskilled ruler that the Romans eventually replaced him with one of their own officials, called a procurator. You probably know the name of the procurator of this region at the time of Jesus' death: Pontius Pilate.

The Realities of the Roman Occupation

Jesus and his companions lived under the rule of a foreign power. The presence of Roman authority was a constant reality, a backdrop to their every activity. They used Roman money and encountered Roman soldiers on the streets. They paid taxes to the emperor as well as local tolls charged on traded goods and for the use of ports, markets, and roads. This money funded useful government building projects but also served to widen the gap between the rich and the poor. Although the Romans were officially tolerant of the many different people they ruled, they also did not hesitate to put down rebellions, often with violence and cruelty. They used the threat of torture and violence to discourage people from challenging Roman power. One of these threats was crucifixion. Crosses with dead and decaying bodies on them lined the road into Jerusalem. The sight was a clear message from the authorities, meant to deter any potential opposition.

pluralistic
Characterized by the presence of many different ethnic, religious, or cultural groups.

Roman Religion

Official Roman religion, which Roman citizens were expected to practice, was based on worship of the emperor as a god. However, by the time of Jesus, many other religious traditions had found their way into Roman culture. These included the Greek gods and goddesses of Mount Olympus and the Egyptian cult of Isis. Even in this **pluralistic** context, Jews existed within the empire as a religious minority.

Live It!

Christ in Society

Jesus encountered opposition to his teachings. Within the Jewish community, many did not recognize him as the promised Messiah and did not see that his teachings fulfilled the Law. Jesus also came in conflict with the Roman leadership and culture.

Similarly, as a follower of Jesus in a world that sometimes values individual freedom over faithfulness to God's will, you may face criticism or opposition because of your faith. You should not lose heart. We have a positive and joyful message to pass on. Pray, set a good example, and talk with your friends. Get involved in action groups, the media, or leadership positions. Rely on the Gifts of the Holy Spirit to overcome the resistance you will face, and bring Christ more into your school, parish, and neighborhood.

How Can This Information Help Us?

We have taken a brief look at the historical, cultural, and political background of Jesus' time. This kind of study can help us to grasp the importance of key aspects of his life and teachings. For example, we see how cruel Herod the Great really was. We can then marvel that Jesus, even as a baby, barely escaped death at the hands of an oppressive ruler. We find out that tax collectors were hated as agents of the Roman occupying forces. We can then appreciate the shock of Jesus' calling tax collectors, like Matthew (see Matthew 9:9) and Zacchaeus (see Luke 19:1–9), to share in his ministry. We learn how the Romans valued violence and militarism and practiced political and economic oppression. We can then grasp the extent to which Jesus challenged Roman society. For example, he proclaimed as blessed the peacemakers, the meek, and the persecuted (see Matthew 5:5,9–10). He also focused his ministry on people on the edges of society. He reached out to women, those who were sick, and those who were poor. Jesus did not compromise in his faithfulness to his mission to begin the Reign of God. This brought him into constant conflict with both political and religious leaders. ✝

This map shows the division of Palestine between the sons of Herod after his death in 4 BC. Archelaeus inherited the areas of Samaria, Judea, and Idumea. Herod Antipas inherited Galilee and Peraea. Philip inherited the regions of Gaulanitis and Batanea in northeastern Palestine.

Article 32 Jesus: Union of the Human and the Divine

hypostatic union
The union of Jesus Christ's divine and human natures in one Divine Person.

At the time appointed by God the Father, the only Son of God, the Eternal Word—that is, the Word and substantial Image of the Father—became incarnate. Without losing his divine nature, he assumed a human nature. In other words, the Son of God, the Second Person of the Trinity, did not stop being God in order to become the man Jesus of Nazareth. Christ was at all times *one* Divine Person with *two* natures. Christians call this the **hypostatic union.** The Greek word *hypostasis* refers to the underlying reality. The two natures do not simply exist one alongside the other; instead, they are joined so completely that both are fully present.

Early Church Councils

In the early centuries of the Church, various heretical beliefs about Jesus were in popular circulation. These heresies included Arianism, which said that Jesus was a kind of in-between creature; he was more than a man but less than God. Another was Nestorianism, which said that in Jesus existed *two separate persons,* one divine and one human. In response to these and other mistaken beliefs, Church councils were convened to define and clarify official Christian teachings about Jesus.

The fourth Ecumenical Council was held at Chalcedon in the year AD 451. It officially established the doctrine of the hypostatic union. The bishops who convened for that event issued a decree summarizing the agreements they had reached.

> We confess that one and the same Christ, Lord, and only-begotten Son, is to be acknowledged in two natures without confusion, change, division, or separation. The distinction between the two natures was never abolished by their union, but rather the character proper to each of the two natures was preserved as they came together in one person *(prosopon)* and one hypostasis.[7] (*CCC,* 467)

A later Ecumenical Council was held in the city of Constantinople in the year AD 553. It further explained this teaching. The gathered bishops maintained that *God* did everything that the *human Jesus* did, including suffering and dying on the cross for us. Because Jesus' divine and human natures cannot be separated, it was not only the human Jesus who endured pain and agony for our redemption; also it was God. The decree produced by the Council of Constantinople states, "He who was crucified in the flesh, our Lord Jesus Christ, is true God, Lord of glory, and *one of the Holy Trinity*"[8] (*CCC*, 468). ✝

Does the Hypostatic Union Matter?

I'll bet if you asked the most faith-filled Catholics you know why they believe in Jesus, they wouldn't answer, "Because of the hypostatic union!" So does all of this Church doctrine, formulated more than fifteen hundred years ago, really matter to our life of faith?

The answer is a definite *yes*. Here's why: Because Jesus is one Divine Person, a union of a fully human nature and a fully divine nature, we know and experience Jesus' divinity *through* his humanity. We come to know Jesus God Made Flesh among us, through knowing Jesus the man. The whole of Jesus' earthly life, including his emotions, friendships, values, and priorities, reveals God to us in a unique and powerful way.

Here's the even more amazing part. When we are baptized as Christians, we are baptized *into* Christ (see Romans 6:3). We become part of Christ's own Body, the Church. Therefore, because of the hypostatic union, we can experience God not only through Jesus' humanity but also through our own humanity. The hypostatic union makes our joys and pains, our triumphs and struggles reveal God, for us and for all those with whom we share our lives.

Pray It!

I Am the Vine

Remain in me, as I remain in you. Just as a branch cannot bear fruit on its own unless it remains on the vine, so neither can you unless you remain in me. I am the vine, you are the branches. Whoever remains in me and I in him will bear much fruit, because without me you can do nothing. (John 15:4–5)

This Scripture passage communicates to us the divine nature of Jesus and his invitation to us for salvation and union with the Father. Read John 15:4–5 prayerfully and reflect on your relationship with Jesus.

Article 33 Jesus: Lord and Redeemer

Lord and Redeemer are two titles often given to Jesus, both in the New Testament and in later writings of the Church Fathers. Understanding the meaning of these two titles can aid our study of Jesus' mission and identity.

Jesus, Our Lord

To understand the significance of calling Jesus "Lord," we need to back up a little. In the Old Testament, most of which was originally written in Hebrew, God reveals the divine name to Moses as YHWH. In Hebrew this name is an unpronounceable form of *to be,* which is often translated as "I am who I am" or "I will be who I will be." Out of respect for the holiness of God's name, both ancient and modern Jewish readers use a different term whenever they see *YHWH.* They use the word *Adonai,* meaning "Lord." When the Old Testament was translated into Greek, the word *Kyrios,* "Lord,"

The divine name YHWH, which God revealed to Moses (see Exodus 3:14), can be literally translated "I am who I am" or "I will be who I will be." What does this divine name say about the nature of God?

© David Lees/CORBIS

was used for the name YHWH. Thus, in the New Testament, giving the title *Kyrios* to Jesus indicates his divinity. When people address Jesus as Lord, it demonstrates not only profound respect and trust but also "the recognition of the divine mystery of Jesus" [9] (*CCC*, 448). Practically speaking, believing in Jesus as our Lord means that all the honor, glory, and reverence we offer to God the Father are due to Jesus as well.

Jesus, Our Redeemer

We also need to back up a little bit to understand the title Redeemer as it applies to Jesus. In the Roman world, a ransom was the price paid to buy the freedom of a slave. The person who paid the ransom was known as a redeemer. Guided by the Holy Spirit, the early Christians began to reflect on the meaning and significance of the death of Jesus, borrowing this language from the Roman world (remember, they were living in the Roman Empire). They were also aware of Old Testament prophecies promising that God would save the people from their sin; see especially some of the promises in Isaiah (43:1–4, 53:1–12). So the early Christians taught that Jesus had "paid the price" to "ransom" us from our slavery to sin; therefore Jesus is truly our Redeemer.

Jesus' death redeemed us from sin (and from death, the consequence of sin) because of the hypostatic union. The hypostatic union is the Christian doctrine that Jesus was one Divine Person with two natures—one human and one divine—fully and completely united. Because Jesus, as the Second Person of the Blessed Trinity, fully assumed our human nature, he was able to redeem that nature through his suffering and death on the cross. What if Jesus had not been fully human? What if, for example, he were only pretending to be human? What if he were God wearing a sort of human disguise, like a costume? Then he would not have been able to redeem us. As the early Church Father Saint Gregory of Nazianzen famously stated, "What was not assumed [in Christ] was not redeemed; whatever is united to God is saved." Jesus completely embraced our human condition, even unto death. He forever united humanity with God and made salvation possible. ✝

Isaiah's Suffering Servant

Each year on Good Friday, the day on which Christians commemorate Jesus' Passion and death, we hear a reading from the prophet Isaiah, which includes these lines:

> Yet it was our infirmities that he bore,
> > our sufferings that he endured,
> While we thought of him as stricken,
> > as one smitten by God and afflicted.
> But he was pierced for our offenses,
> > crushed for our sins.
> Upon him was the chastisement that makes us whole."
>
> > (53:4–5)

This passage is one of four in the prophecy of Isaiah called servant songs (the others are 42:1–7, 49:1–6, and 50:4–9). These songs praise the virtues of an unnamed person who serves God faithfully. He brings justice to the nations even at the cost of great personal suffering.

Biblical scholars have long debated the original identity of this "servant." They wonder if it refers to a specific individual or perhaps collectively to the people of Israel, who had always been invited to serve God faithfully. Early Christians, many of whom were devout Jews, read these passages in light of the life, death, and Resurrection of Jesus. They detected clear parallels between Jesus and the servant. Because they had come to believe in Jesus as their Lord and Redeemer, they interpreted these passages as testimony to the salvific power of Jesus' death, an interpretation that is part of the Church's Tradition.

> Through his suffering, my servant shall justify many,
> > and their guilt he shall bear.
>
> . . . .
>
> He shall take away the sins of many,
> > and win pardon for their offenses.
>
> > (Isaiah 53:11–12)

Part Review

1. Name some examples from the Scriptures that illustrate Jesus' experiencing both the blessings and frustrations of normal life.

2. How do the Gospels help us to understand Jesus' religious life as a faithful Jew?

3. How did the Roman rule in Palestine affect Jesus and the Jewish community?

4. What is the hypostatic union?

5. Why is the hypostatic union important to us today?

6. What does it mean to call Jesus "Lord" and "Redeemer"?

Part 3

Jesus and the Church

Each year at the end of the Easter season, the Church celebrates Pentecost. This feast marks the day when the Holy Spirit came upon the followers of Jesus, enabling them to preach and baptize with the power of Christ. Even today Jesus continues to pour out the Holy Spirit on the Church.

The Church is Christ's own Body in the world. He acts through the Sacraments, which he instituted, bringing us into closer communion with one another and with him. Through the Eucharist, especially, Jesus is present in his Church. He continues his teaching ministry through the Magisterium, or teaching office, of the bishops and the Holy Father. Jesus acts through all the members of the Church as they respond to his will for their lives.

The Church is Christ's own Body in the world. Each of us, in Baptism, has become a member of the Body of Christ and has been given a share in his divine mission as priest, prophet, and king. When we serve others in the name of Jesus, we help to bring his healing, liberating, and redeeming presence to a world in great need of holiness and grace.

The topics covered is this part are:

Article 34 Pentecost and the "New Age" of the Church

The Holy Spirit at Pentecost

After his Resurrection, Jesus appeared to his Apostles and made this promise: "But you will receive power when the holy Spirit comes upon you, and you will be my witnesses in Jerusalem, throughout Judea and Samaria, and to the ends of the earth" (Acts of the Apostles 1:8). So they waited in Jerusalem, along with some of the women disciples, for the Spirit that Jesus had promised. Here's how the story continues:

> And suddenly there came from the sky a noise like a strong driving wind, and it filled the entire house in which they were. Then there appeared to them tongues as of fire, which parted and came to rest on each one of them. And they were all filled with the holy Spirit and began to speak in different tongues, as the Spirit enabled them to proclaim.
>
> Now there were devout Jews from every nation under heaven staying in Jerusalem. At this sound, they gathered in a large crowd, but they were confused because each one heard them speaking in his own language. They were astounded, and in amazement they asked, "Are not all these people who are speaking Galileans? Then how does each of us hear them in his own native language?" (2:2–8)

Catholic Wisdom

The Holy Spirit

Pope Benedict XVI on the Holy Spirit's presence:

We saw once more the grandeur of something which we take too much for granted in our daily lives: the fact that God speaks, that God answers our questions; the fact that, with human words, he speaks to us personally. . . . We realized once again that, in his Word, God is speaking to each one of us, that he speaks to the heart of everyone: if our hearts are alert, and our inner ears are open, we can learn to listen to the word he personally addresses to each of us.

("Address of His Holiness Benedict XVI to the Members of the Roman Curia for the Traditional Exchange of Christmas Greetings")

This event is called Pentecost. It is named for the Jewish feast day on which these events took place. In the Old Testament, Pentecost celebrates God's gift of the Torah, or the Law, to the people of Israel. Now, in the New Testament, Pentecost takes on a new meaning: God gives the Holy Spirit to the community soon to be known as the Church.

The Church Revealed

The *Catechism* explains that the Church was revealed to the world on the day of Pentecost. The Church was founded by Christ, in his preaching, in his healing, and in the saving work of his death, Resurrection, and Ascension. But at Pentecost, the Spirit that had anointed Jesus was now poured out on the Church. The Church became Christ's presence in the world.

We are living in the age of the Church, a time when Christ continues his ministry, not as a historical man living in a particular place and time, but rather through the Church, which is now his true Body. "Christ now lives and acts in and with his Church, in a new way appropriate to this new age" (*CCC*, 1076). ♱

Article 35 Jesus Fulfills His Mission in the Church

After Jesus died, rose, and ascended to Heaven, he was no longer physically present with his followers. However, he gave his disciples, both then and now, the gift of his ongoing presence in the Church, a presence that although not physical is nonetheless real. At Pentecost the followers of Jesus experienced the power of the Holy Spirit. They understood that this power would enable them to continue the work of Jesus through the Church. Gradually the Holy Spirit revealed to the early community of believers that the Church is the true Body of Christ in the world, whose mission is to continue Jesus' ministry. The early community of believers began to understand itself as a Body whose head, and true leader, was Christ himself.

The Church: Goal and Means of God's Plan

The Holy Trinity—Father, Son, and Holy Spirit—has a plan
for the world, and the goal of the plan is the Church. This
doesn't mean that the visible Church as we see it today is that
goal. The Church is a gathering brought about by God's calling people together, but this communion has not been fully
achieved. The Church's journey toward perfection will be
completed only when the Kingdom of God is fully realized
and all the faithful are gathered together in unity with one
another and with God in Heaven.

The Father created the universe out of love for the sake
of this communion of people and their sharing in the divine
life. He sent his Son, Jesus Christ, to forgive sin and make
this communion possible. After Jesus had inaugurated the
Church and all his work on earth was completed, the Holy
Spirit was sent to pour forth gifts upon the Church so that
she can continue Jesus' mission of announcing the Good
News and making disciples. A way of summarizing this is
to say that the Church is the means through which God is
accomplishing his plan, as well as the goal of his plan.

Through the power of the Holy Spirit, Christ has given
the Church four characteristics, or marks. The Church is
One, Holy, Catholic, and Apostolic. The Church is the Body
of Christ; it embodies the same characteristics as Christ himself. Though the Church does not perfectly embody these
characteristics, Christ gives us the grace to grow in attaining
them more completely.

The Church Is One

The Church is One in the Lord. Our founder, Jesus, has
bestowed a unity and common identity upon the baptized.
We are one in the faith that has been passed down from the
apostolic age all the way to the present day. We are also one
in Baptism, the Sacrament that unites all Christians. The
Second Vatican Council's *Decree on Ecumenism* (*Unitatis
Redintegratio,* 1964) states that "all who have been justified by faith in baptism are incorporated into Christ" (3).
This is why we do not baptize those from other Christian
denominations (such as Presbyterians or Methodists) who
want to become Catholic: they are already baptized. As long
as they were baptized with water "in the name of the Father,

and of the Son, and of the Holy Spirit," the Catholic Church embraces them as fellow Christians. Christ's mission is to unite all people in himself; united with Christ through the Church, we are also united with one another.

Images of the Church

Vatican II's *Dogmatic Constitution on the Church* contains a wide variety of images of the Church that speak beautifully and poetically of the profound reality of the gathered people of God:

- The Church is a flock, led by Christ, the Good Shepherd, who gave his life for the sheep.
- The Church is a cultivated field, a fruitful vineyard planted by God in which Christ, the true vine, sustains all the branches.
- The Church is a building made of living stones, constructed by Christ on the foundation of the Apostles.

All of these images are metaphors. Christians are not literally sheep, Christ is not literally a plant, and stones cannot live. However, these symbols speak to us of the great mystery of the Church more deeply than literal language ever could.

The Church Is Holy

As the Body of Christ in the world, the Church is Holy because Christ is unfailingly holy. This mark of the Church does not guarantee the holiness of all the members of the Church. In fact, the *Catechism* states that "all members of the Church, including her ministers, must acknowledge that they are sinners"[10] (827). In recent years the Church has been acutely aware of this. Many allegations of sexual abuse of children by priests and other Church officials have surfaced. It has been painful for us to realize, firsthand, that "perfect holiness is something yet to be acquired" (825). Despite the grave failings of individuals in the Church, the presence of Christ makes it possible for the Church to continue to bring sanctifying grace to the world: "United with Christ, the Church is sanctified by him; through him and with him she becomes sanctifying" (824).

The Church Is Catholic

The Church is Catholic, or universal, in two ways. First, Christ's presence in the Church makes it Catholic; the Church is a body that is unified under one head, Jesus Christ. The Church will be Catholic in this way until the day of Christ's coming again in glory. Second, the Church has a universal mission to the whole human race. The Good News of Jesus Christ is for everyone, not just a select few.

Live It!

Catholic or catholic?

Have you seen the word *catholic* with a lowercase *c*? It is not a typo. The adjective *catholic* comes from the Greek word *katholikós*, meaning "universal" or "comprehensive." When we profess our belief in One, Holy, Catholic, and Apostolic Church, we mean *Catholic* in this broader sense. The Church contains everything needed for salvation. The Church is Catholic because she has a mission from Jesus to the whole world. Everyone, regardless of nationality, race, or age, is welcomed in the Church. The Church is enriched by this diversity.

Where do you see this diversity in your parish or community? Does your parish support a mission church in Africa? Does your pastor regularly say Mass at a local nursing home? The next time you are at church, look for ways you can support this universal mission of the Church.

As members of Christ's Body, we share in Christ's mission to bring all people into unity with him. Though we respect those from other religious traditions, we accept Christ's mandate to "go, therefore, and make disciples of all nations" (Matthew 28:19).

The Church Is Apostolic

The Church is Apostolic. It is "built upon the foundation of the apostles and prophets, with Christ Jesus himself as the capstone" (Ephesians 2:20). With the help of the Holy Spirit, the Church endeavors faithfully to hand on the teaching of the Apostles in every age and circumstance. Moreover, the members of the Church continue to be instructed by the Apostles through their successors, the bishops. ✝

Sacraments
Efficacious and visible signs of God's invisible grace, instituted by Christ. The Seven Sacraments are Baptism, the Eucharist, Confirmation, Penance and Reconciliation, Anointing of the Sick, Matrimony, and Holy Orders.

grace
The gift of God's loving presence with us, which empowers us to respond to his call and to live always as his children. Grace is never earned; although none of us truly deserves grace, God freely chooses to bless us with this gift.

Article 36 Communion with Christ through the Sacraments

Although Christ has ascended into Heaven, he has not left us alone. He "now acts through the sacraments he instituted to communicate his grace" (*CCC*, 1084). When we participate in the **Sacraments,** the Holy Spirit makes Christ present to us. We enter into a closer communion with Christ and one another. Together we become the Body of Christ. The Sacraments allow Christ to live in us. He can work through us, and we can share in his saving work. Sacraments are true encounters with the living Christ, which give us real **grace.** They are often classified into three categories:

- the Sacraments of Christian Initiation (Baptism, Confirmation, the Eucharist)
- the Sacraments of Healing (Anointing of the Sick, Penance and Reconciliation)
- the Sacraments at the Service of Communion (Matrimony, Holy Orders)

All Seven Sacraments allow us to experience Jesus' ongoing presence with his body, the Church, which is "ever-living and life-giving" (*CCC,* 1116).

Visible Signs of an Invisible God

While we live on earth, God's presence is hidden from us.
We cannot see God directly the way we will when we live
in Heaven. The Sacraments allow us to know this invisible
presence of God in visible, tangible ways. In the waters of
Baptism, in the Sacred Chrism (oil) used in Confirmation,
in the words of absolution said by the priest during Penance
and Reconciliation, and in the bread and wine that become
Christ's Body and Blood in the Eucharist, we engage all of
our senses in an experience of God's love and grace. The
various objects, words, gestures, and actions used in each
Sacrament function as sacramental symbols that bring us
God's healing, powerful love. As human beings we need
these physical signs of the presence of a God who never
stops reaching out to us.

Signs of Salvation

The Sacraments, as symbols and rituals, actually put us in
touch with God's power. The Sacraments, most especially the
Eucharist, bring into the present moment the saving action
of Christ. The work of redemption has been accomplished
through the death, Resurrection, and Ascension of Jesus.
The Sacraments bring that saving work into our individual
lives. They offer us new life in Christ.

© Bill Wittman/www.wpwittman.com

For example, the waters of Baptism do
not merely remind us of our new birth
in Christ. We are *really reborn* in those
waters. The words of absolution are
not just something comforting
to say. We are *really forgiven*

Matrimony, or Marriage,
is one of the Seven
Sacraments. How is
Matrimony a visible sign
of God's presence and
love?

when we hear those words. The Eucharist is not just a mental reminder of Christ. The bread and wine *really become* Christ's Body and Blood. They are the *real presence* of Jesus, broken and poured out for the life of the world. Although the Sacraments do celebrate important moments in life, they are much more than that. They empower us to bring the healing power of Jesus' ministry into our everyday lives and to persevere, in faith, through any struggle we face.

Confirmation is one of the Sacraments you might soon be preparing for (or have recently received). When we prepare for Confirmation, we select as a sponsor an adult member of the Church who will help to guide and support us. What traits do you think are important in a sponsor?

© Bill Wittman/www.wpwittman.com

The Ministry of Christ

Though Catholic sacramental celebrations are always led by a minister of the Church (usually a priest, but sometimes a bishop or deacon), in all of the Sacraments, it is really Christ who sanctifies us. For example, it is Christ who baptizes, Christ who confirms, and Christ who gives us his own Body and Blood in the Eucharist—the same Christ who once walked this very earth, living among us and showing us the way to true unity with God and with one another. Our regular participation in the sacramental life of the Church affirms our identity as members of Christ's Body. It strengthens us in holiness and gives us a preview of our heavenly home. ✝

The Sacraments

Sacrament	Essential Sacramental Symbol	Minister	Repeated?
Baptism	Water poured over or immersed in water while saying, "I baptize you in the name of the Father, and of the Son, and of the Holy Spirit"	Bishop, priest, deacon, or anyone in an emergency	No
Confirmation	Laying on of hands and anointing with Chrism (sacred oil) while saying, "Be sealed with the gift of the Holy Spirit"	Bishop or a designated priest	No
Eucharist	Wheat bread and grape wine and the works of consecration	Priest	Yes
Penance and Reconciliation	Laying on of hands and the words of absolution (forgiveness)	Priest	Yes
Anointing of the Sick	Anointing with the oil of the sick accompanied by the liturgical prayer of the priest	Priest	Yes
Holy Orders	Laying on of hands and the prayer of consecration asking for the gifts specific to that order	Bishop	No
Matrimony	Exchange of marriage vows	The couple being married	No, unless a spouse dies

Article 37 Jesus' Presence in the Eucharist

Jesus is uniquely present whenever we celebrate the Eucharist. The Eucharistic **liturgy,** or Mass, is the central liturgy of the Church. *Eucharist* is a Greek word that means "thanksgiving." When we celebrate the Eucharist, we give thanks for all that God has done for us, especially for the Paschal Mystery—Christ's work of salvation accomplished mainly through his Passion, death, Resurrection, and Ascension. Jesus instituted the Eucharist to perpetuate his sacrifice on the cross throughout the ages, until his return in glory—a sacrifice we offer with him at every Mass. The Second Vatican Council's document *Constitution on the Sacred Liturgy*

(*Sacrosanctum Concilium*, 1963) says that Christ is present to us in four ways at a Eucharistic liturgy. He is present in the assembly, in the priest, in the Word, and, most especially, in the **Eucharistic species.** The Eucharist is the heart and summit of the Church's life, because in it Christ unites his Church and all her members with his sacrifice on the cross, offered to God the Father. By this sacrifice he pours out the graces of salvation on his Body, the Church (see *CCC*, 1407).

Christ in the Gathered Assembly

In Matthew's Gospel, Jesus says that "where two or three are gathered together in my name, there am I in the midst of them" (18:20). Therefore Christ is present in the assembly of people when they pray and sing at a Eucharistic liturgy. The next time you are at Mass, think about this: all the people sitting around you are members of Christ's own Body, as are you. In their prayer all are joined to Christ and to one another. At the sign of peace, take the time to look into the eyes of a person as you grasp his or her hand. You and that person have been made one in Christ.

Christ in the Priest

Christ is present in a unique and particular way in the bishop or priest, who presides at a Eucharistic liturgy. As the priest leads us in celebrating the liturgy, he makes the redemptive sacrifice of Christ's death present again for our

liturgy
All official public prayer of the Church, including celebrations of the Eucharist and other Sacraments and the Liturgy of the Hours, the official daily prayers of the Church.

Eucharistic species
The gifts of bread and wine after they have become Christ's Body and Blood.

When we participate in the Eucharist, we take part in the heart and summit of the Church's life. Active participation enables us to more fully experience the presence of Christ. How can you more actively participate in the Mass?

© Bill Wittman/www.wpwittman.com

© Bill Wittman/www.wpwittman.com

salvation. Christ works through the priest to bring the saving power of that death into our lives.

Christ in the Word

Sacred Liturgy states that Christ "is present in his word since it is he himself who speaks when the holy Scriptures are read" (7) during the Mass in the Liturgy of the Word. Christ truly speaks to us through these ancient texts. If we listen carefully and prayerfully, we can gain wisdom, guidance, courage, and peace.

The Body and Blood of Christ

consecrate

Having made a person, place, or thing holy. The Consecration at Mass occurs during the Eucharistic Prayer, when the priest recites Jesus' words of institution, changing the bread and wine into the Body and Blood of Christ.

Jesus is present in a real, substantial, and unique way in his Body and Blood once the bread and wine have been **consecrated.** The Catholic doctrine of the Real Presence means that the elements still taste and look like bread and wine, but they are actually the Body and Blood of Jesus. This is one important aspect of belief where other Christian denominations are not fully united with the Catholic Church. Some denominations teach that Christ is present in the bread and wine only symbolically. Others say the bread and wine are simply reminders of Jesus, the way a treasured gift from a loved one might bring that person to mind. Catholics recognize that although the bread and wine retain their physical forms, they have truly become Jesus' real Body and Blood, and we treat those elements with the utmost care, respect, and reverence at all times. ✝

Pray It!

Eucharistic Adoration

Eucharistic adoration is a type of prayer in which one meditates before the Blessed Sacrament, either privately or during a communal prayer, such as the Benediction. The Blessed Sacrament is the consecrated host, which is the Real Presence of Jesus. Adoration allows us time to simply be with Jesus in a very real way. It will deepen our appreciation for the Mass.

Find out when your parish provides opportunities for Eucharistic adoration and plan to spend one hour in adoration of the Blessed Sacrament. If you do this on a regular basis, you might be surprised at how your relationship with Jesus grows.

"Mass Is Boring!"

Have you ever said this out loud or thought it to yourself? You are not alone. "Mass is boring" tends to be a common complaint of young people. But many adults can also find Eucharistic liturgies to be tedious, unexciting, or unappealing.

The liturgy is the work of the whole Christ, head and body. Thus, the assembly of people gathered for liturgical prayer should be engaged in "full, conscious, and active participation" (*Sacred Liturgy*, 14). Here are a few suggestions for how to do that:

- Sing and make the appropriate spoken responses, like "Amen" and "Thanks be to God."

- Pray the words of the liturgy by focusing your attention on the readings and prayers.

- Read and reflect on the Scripture readings before going to Mass.

- Become a liturgical minister, like an altar server, lector, cantor, or Eucharistic minister.

- Recognize the great gift the Eucharist offers to us. We cannot guarantee that every liturgical celebration will be exciting or even enjoyable. We can guarantee that every liturgy will offer us abundant grace and the real presence of Christ. Excitement or enjoyment aside, that is a marvelous, and definitely not boring, truth.

Article 38 Jesus Teaches through the Church

Think of the best teachers you've ever had. What was so great about them? Did they know their subject matter? Could they explain concepts clearly and well? Did they care about the students? Jesus had all of these traits and more. He was the greatest of all teachers.

In the four Gospels, Jesus is called "Teacher" forty-five times. (The Hebrew word for teacher is *rabbi*.) This reflects his frequent practice of teaching the crowds of people who follow him from place to place. For example, look at Matthew's Sermon on the Mount. (It begins in 5:2.) Jesus teaches about anger, prayer, divorce, and the Golden Rule. In Mark's Gospel, Jesus teaches the crowd out of concern for them: "When he disembarked and saw the vast crowd, his heart was moved with pity for them, for they were like sheep without a shepherd; and he began to teach them many things" (6:34). Another time Jesus teaches the people in his hometown synagogue. They are so impressed that "all spoke highly of him and were amazed at the gracious words that came from his mouth" (Luke 4:22). After hearing one of Jesus' parables, Jesus' listeners "were astonished at his teaching, for he taught them as one having authority, and not as their scribes" (Matthew 7:28–29).

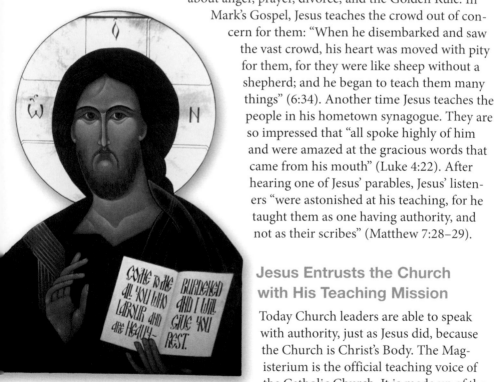

© Bill Wittman/www.wpwittman.com

"[Jesus] said to them again, 'Peace be with you. As the Father has sent me, so I send you'" (John 20:21). Jesus entrusted his disciples to carry on his teaching mission. Through Apostolic Succession this mission has been entrusted to the Church today.

Jesus Entrusts the Church with His Teaching Mission

Today Church leaders are able to speak with authority, just as Jesus did, because the Church is Christ's Body. The Magisterium is the official teaching voice of the Catholic Church. It is made up of the Pope and the bishops, the successors of Peter and the Apostles, who speak with one global, unified voice. The Magisterium issues pronouncements on matters of Catholic doctrine, as well as on certain moral questions.

When the bishops exercise their ministry of teaching, they follow the example of Christ the Teacher, the one who gave the Apostles and their successors the authority to teach in his name. As the *Catechism* states, the bishops are "authentic teachers—that is, teachers endowed with the authority of Christ, who preach the faith to the people entrusted to them, the faith to be believed and put into practice"[11] (2034). The Magisterium is entrusted with handing on and interpreting the truth revealed by God through the Scriptures and Tradition.

Infallibility

When the Pope issues a pronouncement *ex cathedra* (a Latin phrase that literally means "from the chair"), his words are considered to be infallible—that is, without error. The bishops, when speaking with one unified voice together with the Pope, also share in this gift of infallibility. As Vatican II's *Dogmatic Constitution on the Church* states, the bishops "proclaim Christ's doctrine infallibly" when in their authoritative teaching concerning matters of faith and morals, "they are in agreement on one position as definitively to be held" (25). The *Catechism* further explains that the infallibility of the Magisterium "extends to all the elements of doctrine, including moral doctrine, without which the saving truths of the faith cannot be preserved, expounded, or observed" (2051). Infallibility is a gift of Christ to the Church. It is a guarantee that we will continue to have access to the truth necessary for our salvation until Christ comes again in glory.
✝

Article 39 Jesus' Ministry through the Community of Faith

Our Baptism makes us members of Christ's own Body. As such, we share in Christ's mission as priest, prophet, and king. Have you ever been to a liturgy at which the Sacrament of Baptism was celebrated? You may recall hearing this prayer just before the person was anointed: "The God of power and Father of our Lord Jesus Christ has freed you from sin and brought you to new life through water and the Holy Spirit. He now anoints you with the chrism of salvation,

evangelical counsels

The call to go beyond the minimum rules of life required by God (such as the Ten Commandments and the precepts of the Church) and strive for spiritual perfection through a life marked by a commitment to chastity, poverty, and obedience.

so that, united with his people, you may remain for ever a member of Christ, who is Priest, Prophet, and King" (*The Rite of Baptism,* 62).

As the community of baptized people who bear the name of Christ, we participate in the ongoing ministry of Christ to the world through the particular vocation to which God has called us. All Christian vocations are oriented to service, whether through ordained ministry, through the consecrated life, or as a member of the laity.

Ordained Ministry

Ordained ministry as a bishop, priest, or deacon is conferred through the Sacrament of Holy Orders. Bishops are in charge of a particular geographical region of the Church called a diocese or archdiocese. Deacons and priests assist the bishop in caring for the needs of the Church within that region. You are probably most familiar with priests, who serve at your parish and perhaps at your school. A priest's unique role is sacramental ministry, especially presiding at Eucharistic liturgies and celebrations of the Sacrament of Penance and Reconciliation. Many priests have promised to serve God's people in obedience to a bishop within a certain diocese. These are called diocesan priests. Other priests are members of religious orders, such as the Jesuits, the Franciscans, or the Dominicans. These priests are not tied to one diocese. They may travel throughout the world, usually to places where members of their religious order serve. In the ministry of priests, Christ the Healer, Liberator, and Redeemer continues his work.

The Laity: Marriage, Parenthood, and Single Life

The vast majority of Christians live out their baptismal call to service as a member of the laity. Technically a layperson is anyone who is not ordained, but this term is commonly used to refer to anyone who is neither ordained nor a member of a religious order.

Laypeople who are called to Marriage serve God through a loving, self-sacrificial relationship with their spouse, and, if God wills that they become parents, their children. Other laypeople are called to a dedicated (or committed) single life, which allows them the freedom to help their parents, siblings, and other family members and to engage in works of charity and justice. In the care and generosity of the laity, Christ, who was perfect love for our salvation, continues his work.

Consecrated Life

Some Christian laity are also called to live the consecrated life. The consecrated life is a permanent state of life that is marked by the following three lifelong commitments, which are also called **evangelical counsels:**

- a commitment to *poverty,* to limit their ownership and use of material possessions, focusing on people instead of things
- a commitment to *chastity,* to serve only God with their whole heart, mind, and soul, refraining from marriage and from romantic relationships
- a commitment to *obedience,* to listen carefully to God's will for their lives and to serve wherever they are needed

There are many different ways of living the consecrated life. Some people are called to live as hermits, separating themselves from all the cares and distractions of the world so they can completely commit themselves to prayer, penance, and meditation. Some are called to live as consecrated virgins or consecrated widows, still living in the world and devoting themselves to a life of prayer, penance, and service. These people are consecrated to God by their diocesan bishop, in an approved liturgical rite.

© Bill Wittman/www.wpwittman.com

Just as each one of us is unique, we are each called to our own unique vocation. Whether we are called to married, ordained, consecrated, or single life, we share a common mission to be Christ for the world.

VOWS

Promises made to God.

The majority of those living the consecrated life serve as members of a religious order (sometimes called a religious community or congregation). These individuals are often called "Sister" or "Brother." You may know about a few of the hundreds of Catholic religious orders, such as the Marianists, the Sisters of Mercy, the Daughters of Charity, the De La Salle Christian Brothers, and the Fathers and Brothers of the Holy Cross. The ministry of most religious orders focuses on meeting some particular need, such as education, health care, or service to the poor. All members of religious orders take public **vows** to live the evangelical counsels.

In the faithful service of those who live the consecrated life, Christ, the Compassion of God poured out for the life of the world, continues his work. ✝

Part Review

1. Describe the significance of Pentecost for the Church.

2. The Church is both the means and the goal of God's saving plan. What does this mean?

3. What are the four characteristics, or marks, of the Church? What does each tell us about the Church?

4. What three categories are often used to classify the Seven Sacraments?

5. How do the Sacraments bring the saving action of Christ into our lives?

6. Name four ways Jesus is present in a celebration of the Eucharistic liturgy.

7. What does the Catholic doctrine of the Real Presence mean?

8. What is the Magisterium?

9. What are the vocations through which Christians share in the ministry of Christ?

Jesus: The Definitive Revelation of God's Plan

Part 1

Jesus Reveals a Vision of Authentic Humanity

What does it mean to be a human being? What are our human responsibilities and duties? How should we treat other people? How should we treat the earth? People have asked questions like these since we first discovered and developed our capacity for thought. Every culture and society has had its own perspective on these and other basic issues of human identity.

As Catholics we answer these questions in light of our faith in Jesus Christ. All of Christ's life, his teachings, his actions, his miracles, his death, and his Resurrection teach us who we are and how we are to live. Because the Eternal Son of God fully assumed human nature, we can look to him for a vision of authentic humanity. Jesus invites us to follow his example of a humble life devoted to prayer and service. He also calls us to use our God-given gifts of intellect and free will as we seek to love all people, including our enemies, and to care responsibly for all creation.

The topics covered is this part are:

- Article 40: "What Does It Mean to Be Fully Human?" (page 135)

- Article 41: "The Gifts of Intellect and Free Will" (page 137)

- Article 42: "To Love and Be Loved" (page 140)

- Article 43: "The Call to Be Stewards of Creation" (page 142)

40 What Does It Mean to Be Fully Human?

Jesus Christ, the Eternal Son of God, fully assumed human nature and lived an earthly life. All of Christ's life was a continual teaching—his speeches, his miracles, his prayers, his interactions with his disciples, his love for people, his special care for the poor, his total sacrifice on the cross for the redemption of all people, and his Resurrection. All the events of his life are the "actualization of his word and the fulfillment of Revelation" (*Catechism of the Catholic Church [CCC]*, 561).

Made in the Image of God

To be fully human is to be aware of our identity as people made in God's image (see Genesis 1:27). Being made in God's image does not mean we physically look like God, the way children resemble their parents. Nor does it mean we necessarily act like God all the time; we all sin and make mistakes. Rather, it means we have a fundamental dignity and we are predestined to reproduce the image of God's Son made man, the "'image of the invisible God' (*Col* 1:15)" (*CCC*, 381).

Jesus responded to the dignity of others. He never treated them as things but always as people made in the divine image. He sought out and ministered to those whose dignity was not recognized in the society of his day. He healed lepers, treated sinners with respect, and reached out to Samaritans and to Gentiles. All of these were people whom many Jews of Jesus' time would look down on. Jesus ministered to these people whom society pushed aside. He made it clear that everyone has an inherent, or built-in, dignity given to them by the Creator.

Jesus, Our Model

Not only did Jesus teach us about the inherent dignity of all persons, he also embodied all that is good in humanity. Therefore, "in all of his life Jesus presents himself as *our model*. He is 'the perfect man,'[1] who invites us to become his disciples and follow him. In humbling himself, he has given us an example to imitate, through his prayer he draws us to pray, and by his poverty he calls us to accept freely the privation and persecutions that may come our way"[2] (*CCC*, 520). Let's explore each of the points mentioned here as we try to understand how Jesus is a model for us.

- *Humility.* The Son of God humbles himself simply by assuming human nature. However, one clear example of Jesus' humility in his earthly life occurs in John's Gospel. At the Last Supper, he washes the disciples' feet (see 13:1–20). Washing feet, a traditional sign of service and hospitality, was normally performed by a slave. Yet Jesus, the "teacher" and "master" (13:13), takes on this task. He gives his disciples an example of humble service and a vision of God's Reign. Indeed he explicitly tells the disciples, "I have given you a model to follow, so that as I have done for you, you should also do" (13:15).

- *Prayer.* In praying numerous times throughout the Gospels, Jesus models for us a life firmly grounded in a relationship with God the Father. He also teaches us to pray in the words of the Lord's Prayer, or the Our Father (see Luke 11:2–4, Matthew 6:9–13).

- *Poverty.* From his birth in humble surroundings to his death on the cross, Jesus lived and died in material poverty. For much of his public ministry, Jesus did not even have a permanent home: "Foxes have dens and birds of the sky have nests, but the Son of Man has nowhere to rest his head" (Matthew 8:20). Jesus thus challenges us to consider our relationship to material things and our willingness to do without certain physical comforts. ✝

Pray It!

Care for Others

Dear Jesus,
Encourage us to care less about things and more about other people. Teach us to be willing to make sacrifices so we can use our time and money to help those in need. Help us to forget our own comfort so we can more readily provide for the relief of others. May your life inspire us to be generous and compassionate at all times. In your name we pray. Amen.

A Hymn about Christ

Saint Paul's letter to the Philippians contains a beautiful early Christian hymn about the humility of Jesus and our call to imitate it. It reads, in part, as follows:

> Have among yourselves the same attitude that is also yours in Christ Jesus,
>
>> Who, though he was in the form of God,
>>> did not regard equality with God something to be grasped.
>>> Rather, he emptied himself,
>>> taking the form of a slave,
>>> coming in human likeness;
>>> and found human in appearance,
>>> he humbled himself,
>>> becoming obedient to death, even death on a cross.
>
> (2:5–8)

This passage powerfully expresses the Christian call to humility, as exemplified by the life and death of Jesus. Because the Son of God willingly gave up his right to remain "in the form of God" (2:6), we must be willing to put aside our own needs and engage in loving, generous service of others. Often this work is not glamorous. We may never receive a reward or recognition for our labor. But we will know that we are following in the path of Jesus, the One whose life and death of humble, obedient service brought salvation to all the world.

Article 41 The Gifts of Intellect and Free Will

The vision of authentic humanity revealed for us by Jesus includes the gifts of intellect and free will.

Intellect

What intellectual abilities do we have? We have the capacity to think and reason logically and to learn about the world around us. We also have the ability to make wise decisions and to think about the consequences of our actions. Of all God's creation, only human beings can develop these wonderful skills! Paragraph 15 of Vatican II's *Pastoral Constitution on the Church in the Modern World* (*Gaudium et Spes*, 1965)

conscience

A person's God-given internal sense of what is morally right or wrong. To make good judgments, a person needs to have a well-formed conscience.

describes the human intellect as a "sharing in the light of the divine mind." It praises human "attempts to search out the secrets of the material universe" and draws attention to the progress we have made "in the empirical sciences, in technology, and in the liberal arts." Indeed, when people research to discover the cure for a disease, when they think carefully about how to bring peace between two warring nations, or when they plan and create a beautiful work of art, they are using the intellectual powers God has blessed them with.

Paragraph 15 of *The Church in the Modern World* also makes clear that through the power of the Holy Spirit, we are able to use our intellectual abilities to pursue "truths of a higher order": the truths of divine wisdom. Wisdom "gently draws the human mind to look for and to love what is true and good." Ultimately, wisdom leads us to God: "We are led through visible realities to those which are invisible."

Free Will

God always wants us to make good, morally correct decisions. His grace prepares our heart to respond to him and recognize the good, even before we make a moral decision. God gives each of us a **conscience** to help us to choose rightly. However, he has also given us the gift of freedom, or free will, to choose our own path in life. This means God cannot force us to act a certain way. Think about it: Could you force someone to love you? If a person says he or she loves you or acts like he or she loves you, it is not really love

Live It!

Serving with Your Mind

One way you can do the will of God right now is by being the best student you can be. God gave you intellectual abilities so you could be fully human and give glory to him. How? By developing them as best you can and using them to serve others.

You can develop your intellect by seeing how your academic studies relate to God's actions. The sciences that explore the nature of the universe, for example, show the wonderful order and beauty of God's creative work. Literature and social studies show the drama of how human beings, the summit of creation, have used their God-given freedom to do good or evil.

Through your studies you can develop such skills as logical thinking, critical reading, and careful communication. All of these will help you to serve others, whatever your vocation.

if you have to force the person to say that or to act like that. Similarly, God cannot force us to love him or to do the right thing. It is our free choice. God wills that we try our very best to live in loving harmony with other people and with all creation, but in the end, the choice is ours. If we choose to open ourselves to divine grace, the Holy Spirit can help us to use our free will wisely with strength and courage.

Even Jesus, when his death was right around the corner, was free to choose whether to follow through with what God the Father wanted of him. In Mark's Gospel, Jesus prays that the "cup" of suffering he is about to endure might pass

Catholic Colleges and Universities

You may have attended a Catholic elementary school. You now attend a Catholic high school. Did you know you can continue your Catholic education in college? The Catholic Church holds the intellectual pursuit of academic knowledge and spiritual wisdom in high esteem. The heart of this Catholic intellectual life is found in Catholic colleges and universities. Catholic universities have flourished in Europe since the Middle Ages. The first Catholic institution of higher education in the United States was founded in 1787. Today in the United States, 245 Catholic colleges and universities enroll more than 600,000 students each year.

Every Catholic college or university is unique, but they all view our intellectual abilities as gifts from God. This understanding of the divine origin of the human intellect informs the approach to every academic subject, from art to biology, from physics to philosophy. Indeed, developing our abilities in a wide variety of fields of study is a gift we can offer back to the God who has given so much to us.

© Ardress/shutterstock.com

Samaritans

Residents of Samaria, the central hill country of Palestine. In the time of Jesus, tremendous ethnic hatred and tension, which sometimes erupted into violence, existed between Jews and Samaritans.

him by. Yet, he also prays "not what I will but what you will" (14:36). In this way he models for us perfect obedience—freely choosing to surrender to God's will and desire for our lives. ✝

Article 42 To Love and Be Loved

In his life, death, and Resurrection, Jesus reveals that we have been created to love. We are to love God, and, because we love God, we are to love our neighbor (see *CCC,* 1822). No other creature on earth can offer to the Creator the "response of faith and love" that we can (357).

How Did Jesus Love?

Jesus loved others in every aspect of his earthly ministry. As a teacher he loved by speaking the truth. He did so even when people were reluctant to listen to him and even when they threatened him with violence. As a healer he loved by making the lame walk, the blind see, the deaf hear, and the dead rise. As the one who was the Word of divine mercy incarnate, he loved by seeking out those whom society had excluded and forgotten, like those who were poor, the **Samaritans,** and women. Jesus welcomed people like this—people with little power, influence, or worldly success—to be his friends and followers.

Most of all, Jesus loved others through his death. In fidelity to the will of his Divine Father, he willingly gave himself so that all people might be free from sin and death. When we follow the example of Jesus' self-sacrificial love, we are well on our way to full humanity. We are becoming the people God has always desired us to be.

How Does Jesus Want Us to Love?

Jesus invites us to love because God the Father first loved him. As God the Father, the First Person of the Blessed Trinity, loves Jesus, so Jesus loves his disciples, and so we are to love one other. As Jesus states in John's Gospel, shortly before his arrest: "As the Father loves me, so I also love you. Remain in my love. . . . This is my commandment: love one another as I love you. No one has greater love than this, to lay down one's life for one's friends" (15:9,12–13).

Laying down one's life for one's friends might seem like a tall order, but it is the heart of Christian love. Many popular songs lead us to think love is a happy, warm feeling. In reality love is a choice. When we choose to love other people, we choose to love them even when they disappoint us or even when we realize they are not perfect. We choose to seek their

Sr. Helen Prejean

"Is God vengeful, demanding a death for a death? Or is God compassionate, luring souls into love so great that no one can be considered 'enemy'?"

So writes Sr. Helen Prejean, a leading Catholic advocate for the abolition of the death penalty. Sister Helen was born in 1939 in Baton Rouge, Louisiana. She joined the Sisters of Saint Joseph of Medaille at the age of eighteen and worked as an educator for many years. In 1981 she began corresponding with a death-row inmate, who asked her to be his spiritual advisor and to be with him when he was put to death. Sister Helen agreed. Her experience of accompanying him through the months leading up to his execution deeply changed the course of her life. She began to speak out against capital punishment. Her stance was rooted in her firm belief that all people, even those who have done horrible things, have a God-given right to live, to love, and to be loved by others.

Sister Helen has since served as a spiritual advisor to other death-row inmates, and she has written two books about her experiences in this ministry. She has also started a group to serve the needs of the families of murder victims.

Sister Helen's life and work witness to the power of the choice to love others. She invites us to consider these questions: Who are the people we consider unlovable? Can we remember that God loves these people? Can we pray for the grace to love them too?

parables
Stories rooted in daily life that use symbolism or allegory as a teaching tool and that usually have a surprise ending.

stewards
People who are put in charge of managing, caring for, and protecting something, such as money or personal property.

good, even at the expense of our own comfort or sometimes even our own lives.

Jesus invites us to choose to love even our enemies: "Love your enemies, and pray for those who persecute you, that you may be children of your heavenly Father" (Matthew 5:44–45). With the help of the Holy Spirit, we can make this choice to love even those who have hurt us greatly. We can recognize that these people are beloved of God too. If we could see our enemies as God sees them, what would we see? ☩

Article 43 The Call to Be Stewards of Creation

Jesus lived closely in touch with the natural world. Many of his disciples were farmers, fishers, and shepherds—people whose livelihood depended on the land and the sea. In his **parables** he told stories about planting seeds, losing sheep, gathering a harvest, and hauling in a catch. These and other activities he referred to were familiar to his listeners. Jesus knew that humanity and the natural world are deeply interconnected. This reveals our call to care for creation responsibly.

The Creator's Gift

As the Creator of all the earth, "God willed the diversity of his creatures and their own particular goodness, their interdependence, and their order" (*CCC,* 353). According to the design of God, *"each creature possesses its own particular goodness and perfection,"* reflecting "in its own way a ray of God's infinite wisdom and goodness" (339). This vast universe in which we make our home is God's gracious gift to us, for he "destined all material creatures for the good of the human race" (353). By caring for the natural world and allowing it to sustain us in life, we enable all of creation to share in the glory of the One who is the Source of all being.

The Goods of the Earth: Intended for All

We are used to thinking of the things we own as "mine." My room, my clothes, my cell phone, my posters, and so on. It is easy to get possessive and forget that all the material things we own ultimately come from God. He allows us to own and use them but wants us to be aware of the rights and needs of others.

Because the earth is the "original gift" of God to humanity (*CCC*, 2403), the goods of the earth—like land, water, air, food, and energy—are the rightful property of all people and are destined for the whole human race. The earth is divided among all people to assure the security and dignity of human lives. To deny anyone access to the goods of the earth is to steal, and is a violation of the Seventh Commandment. All people have a right to private possessions and property acquired in a just way, for guaranteeing their freedom and dignity and helping them meet their basic needs and the needs of those in their care. However, we must assert this right to private property while also working to ensure that all people can have their basic needs met and live in dignity. We must follow the "practice of justice and charity in the administration of earthly goods" (2451). God is the ultimate source of all we have. We are obligated to make sure that all people enjoy a share in the many good things of the earth.

Our Call to Stewardship

In the Creation stories of Genesis, God tells the newly created men and women to "have dominion over the fish of the sea, the birds of the air, and all the living things that move on the earth" (1:28). Sometimes people mistakenly think the word *dominion* gives us permission to do whatever we want to creation—that it is here simply for us to use and enjoy. However, the *Catechism* states that dominion "is not to be an arbitrary and destructive domination" (373); rather, we are to be **stewards** of all life, including human life, and of the

Catholic Wisdom

Saint Francis and the World

Why did Saint Francis call created things his brothers and sisters? Saint Bonaventure, a Franciscan and a Doctor of the Church, wrote this about Saint Francis: "He saw God in everything, and loved and praised him in all creation. . . . The realization that everything comes from the same source made him call all created things—no matter how insignificant—his brothers and sisters, because they had the same origins as he."

earth itself. Using the word *steward* to describe the sacred relationship between humanity and creation reminds us that we are never to exploit creation or use it for our benefit only; rather, we must safeguard it in a way that acknowledges its goodness and preserves it for future generations. This

Saint Francis of Assisi: Patron of Ecology

Saint Francis was born in Assisi, in modern-day Italy. He lived in the late twelfth and early thirteenth centuries. Francis was born into wealth, and his father expected him to go into the family cloth business. However, Francis felt called to serve the poor of his hometown, especially beggars and lepers. Once while praying, Francis had a vision of the Crucified Christ. Christ told him, "Francis, Francis, go and repair my house which, as you can see, is falling into ruins." Shortly after this Francis gave up his right to inherit his father's goods. He gave himself over to a life of poverty. He later founded the Franciscans, a religious order of priests, broth-ers, and sisters who continue to serve God's people—especially the poor—today.

There is a long tradition that has associated Saint Francis with nature, espe-cially animals. Pope John Paul II recognized this and formally made Saint Francis the patron of ecology in 1979. Saint Francis's famous poem "Canticle of the Creatures" reveals his close relationship with the natural world, for he praises "brother sun," "sister moon," "brother fire," and "sister water." On his feast day, October 4, many Catholic churches bless pets and other animals, asking God, through the intercession of Saint Francis, to protect and care for them.

"religious respect for the integrity of creation"[3] (*CCC*, 2415) helps us to see the care of creation as a crucial part of our vocation. God has commanded us to care for that which is his gift to us. ✝

Part Review

1. What does it mean that human beings are made in God's image?

2. How is Jesus a model of full humanity for us?

3. Describe the gifts of intellect and free will and explain how God wants us to use them.

4. How did Jesus model love for us?

5. How does Jesus want us to love?

6. In what ways does stewardship describe the relationship humans are to have with the earth?

Part 2

Jesus Reveals Our Inherent Dignity

In order to save us by reconciling us with God, Jesus Christ, the Eternal Son of God, fully assumed our human nature in the Incarnation. He restored the image of God in us, an image that sin had tarnished. Through the mystery of his Passion, death, Resurrection, and Ascension, he redeemed us, offering us a share in the communion of the Blessed Trinity even while we live on earth. He ensured our ultimate destiny: eternal life in the glory of God's holy presence. Finally, Jesus revealed our inherent human dignity.

As we seek to honor this fundamental human dignity, we must remember that all people have been created in the image and likeness of God and redeemed by the saving work of Jesus Christ. We must acknowledge women and men as equal partners, meant to serve the Creator side by side. We also must uphold the sanctity of all human life, at all its stages, from conception to natural death.

The topics covered is this part are:

Article 44 Created, Redeemed, and Bound For Glory

The heart of human dignity consists of three fundamental truths: (1) we are created as good, (2) we are in need of salvation, and (3) we are meant for eternal life in the glory of God's holy presence.

Created as Good

The opening chapter of the Book of Genesis states that humanity has been created in the image and likeness of God (see 1:26–27). As creatures who occupy this "unique place in creation" (*CCC,* 355), we have a dignity that can never be taken away from us. The Incarnation—the event in which God became flesh—further affirms the basic goodness of the world in general, and of humanity in particular. If the world were not good, God would not have come to live in the world. If humanity were not good, God would never have assumed human nature and lived among us as Jesus of Nazareth.

Saint Augustine versus Pelagius

Saint Augustine, Bishop of Hippo in North Africa, and Pelagius, a British monk, fought for years over an important theological controversy in the fifth century. The matter concerned a basic question of human identity: Can we do good on our own, or do we always need the help of God's grace to do good?

Pelagius believed that we are capable of doing good by ourselves, without the benefit of grace. He maintained that we can use our free will to pray, love others, engage in works of service and justice, and follow God's will. Pelagius even thought it is possible not to sin at all if we just try hard enough.

In contrast, Saint Augustine believed that Original Sin left humanity permanently wounded. Therefore, we cannot do good on our own. However, God's grace supports us in our weakness and enables us to choose the good. We may think we have made our own choice to do good, but Saint Augustine would say that God planted the desire for good in our hearts. Saint Augustine recognized that God's abundant and powerful grace always comes first.

After years of controversy, the Church acknowledged that Saint Augustine correctly understood human nature: We are created as good but are in constant need of redemptive grace. Pelagius's views were judged to be heretical, or false.

In Need of Redemption

Although humanity was created fundamentally good, we are in need of redemption because of **the Fall.** In the Fall, sin first entered the world, and it has been a part of our human experience ever since. This fallen nature, transmitted to every person born into the world, is called Original Sin. "Adam and Eve committed a *personal sin*, but this sin affected *the human nature* that they would then transmit *in a fallen state*"[4] (*CCC,* 404). The doctrine of Original Sin does not mean we are born with personal faults. Rather, it means we enter the world "wounded," "inclined to sin" (405), and in need of redemption. Original Sin makes it hard for us to say no to temptation and inclines us to act for our own selfish pleasures rather than to do what is right.

Our redemption flows from God's initiative of love for us, because "he loved us and sent his Son as expiation for our sins" (1 John 4:10). Jesus freely offered himself for our salvation, and through his Passion, death, Resurrection, and Ascension, we can be redeemed. Saint Paul explains that Jesus' fidelity to the will of his Divine Father essentially undoes the sin of Adam: "Just as through one person sin entered the world, and through sin, death, and thus death came to all . . . if by that one person's transgression the many died, how much more did the grace of God and the gracious gift of the one person Jesus Christ overflow for the many" (Romans 5:12,15). The Exultet is the Church's song of thanksgiving prayed at the Great Vigil of Easter. It further

Pray It!

In My Father's House

At the Last Supper, Jesus said to the Apostles: "In my Father's house there are many dwelling places. If there were not, would I have told you that I am going to prepare a place for you? And if I go and prepare a place for you, I will come back again and take you to myself, so that where I am you also may be. Where [I] am going you know the way" (John 14:2–4). Thomas responded with a question: "Master, we do not know where you are going; how can we know the way?" (14:5). Have you ever felt that way about your faith life?

Jesus gave a very straightforward answer to Thomas's question: "I am the way and the truth and the life. No one comes to the Father except through me. If you know me, then you will also know my Father" (14:6–7). The next time you pray, reflect on Jesus' response to Thomas and pray to know Jesus better.

explains this connection between Adam and Christ: "O truly necessary sin of Adam, destroyed completely by the Death of Christ! / O happy fault that earned so great, so glorious a Redeemer!" *(Roman Missal)*. Through Baptism we access the grace of this great Redeemer, Jesus, who heals the wounds of our sins and turns us back toward God (see *CCC*, 405).

Bound for Glory

We have been created as good and redeemed by Christ. This fact ensures our ultimate destiny: eternal life in the glory of God's holy presence. Jesus reveals this when he states: "In my Father's house there are many dwelling places. If there were not, would I have told you that I am going to prepare a place for you?" (John 14:2–3). Similarly, the First Letter of John states that "we shall be like him, for we shall see him as he is" (3:2). The scriptural witness is clear: we have a heavenly home. Sharing in the sacramental life of the Church enables us to attain this ultimate destiny and strengthens us on our journey toward it. The Sacraments reinforce our fundamental identity: We are human persons destined to share in the eternal glory of the One who created us in perfect goodness and redeemed us in perfect love. ✝

Fall, the
Also called the Fall from Grace, the biblical revelation about the origins of sin and evil in the world, expressed figuratively in the story of Adam and Eve in Genesis.

immortal
Living forever; not subject to death.

Article 45 The Inherent Dignity of All People

The Book of Genesis tells us that God is the Creator of the whole world, including people. All of creation—plants and trees, animals and birds, sun and moon—has come from God, but only humans are created in the divine image. This is the root of a central truth about humanity: All of us— women, men, and children of every race, language, age, and way of life—have a unique, inherent dignity given to us by God. *Inherent* means that this dignity is so much a part of us that no one can ever take it away.

Body and Soul United

In creating us with inherent dignity, God has fashioned humanity as truly unique, for only we have a spiritual, **immortal** soul. Though our parents provide the genetic

Saint Katharine Drexel

Saint Katharine Drexel was born in Philadelphia, Pennsylvania, in 1858. She was the daughter of a successful banker. She used her enormous inheritance to establish schools for Native Americans and African Americans. At this time in history, nearly a century before the civil rights movement, these groups were still overcoming a legacy of oppression and slavery. They were often the victims of prejudice and did not have access to education. Yet Saint Katharine saw their inherent dignity. In 1891 she founded a new religious order, the Sisters of the Blessed Sacrament, specifically devoted to educating Native Americans and African Americans. In the course of her lifetime, Katharine founded more than two hundred schools and missions to serve these groups. She also played a significant role in establishing Xavier University in New Orleans. It was the first and only predominantly African-American Catholic University.

Saint Katharine was able to see all people—even those whom society viewed as inferior—as God sees them. How can *you* challenge others to recognize and respond to the inherent dignity of all people?

© Bettmann/CORBIS

material that grows into our physical bodies, our souls are created directly by God. While we live on earth, our bodies and souls dwell together, as one unified being. Indeed "it is because of its spiritual soul that the body made of matter becomes a living, human body" (*CCC,* 365). When we die, our souls separate from our bodies. At the final resurrection, our souls will be reunited with our glorified, resurrected bodies.

Not Some*thing*, but Some*one*

The *Catechism* states that "being in the image of God the human individual possesses the dignity of a person, who is not just something, but someone" (357). What does the phrase "not just something, but someone" mean? It means we cannot treat people as objects or use them for our own purposes. Such abuse of human persons is a grave violation of the dignity God has given them.

This is why, during his lifetime, Jesus treated every person he met—including sinners, outcasts, those who were sick, and those who were poor—with care and compassion. Jesus looked beyond the limits that so often stop us from seeing the dignity of others. For example, we read in the Bible that Jesus engages in a lengthy conversation with a Samaritan woman even though she is a member of a group the Jews reject (see John 4:4–42). He heals the servant of a Roman official even though Romans are hated as the foreign occupying power in Judea (see Matthew 8:5–13). He cures the daughter of a Canaanite woman even though his disciples urge him to send her away (see Matthew 15:21–28). The people Jesus lived with commonly viewed Samaritans, Romans, and Canaanites with suspicion, but Jesus treated them with kindness, respect, and concern.

The Catholic Church seeks to follow the example of Jesus by protecting the dignity of every human person. Vatican II's *The Church in the Modern World* states that "every

Live It!

Respecting Others

How challenging is it to act with respect for others around your school? It can be difficult sometimes to recognize the dignity of people we encounter in our daily lives. It might be because they don't treat us with respect, or maybe we are just busy and forget. As you start your school day or encounter people throughout the day, ask yourself the following questions:

- Do I try to greet others in a friendly and welcoming manner?
- Do I treat everyone fairly and avoid judging or disregarding people who are different from me?
- Do I avoid prejudging people based on how they look, their intelligence, or who their friends are?
- Do I look for the good in each person I encounter?
- Do I try to get to know and understand people I don't know or people I disagree with?

When we make an effort to treat everyone in a way that respects their God-given dignity, we can discover the good that is in them. Everyone is a child of God and worthy of respect.

form of social or cultural discrimination in fundamental personal rights on the grounds of sex, race, color, social conditions, language, or religion must be curbed and eradicated as incompatible with God's design"[5] (*CCC*, 1935). Therefore, the Church consistently speaks out against racism, sexism, abortion, human trafficking, and other oppressive, discriminatory practices. ✞

Article 46 In the Image and Likeness of God

The Book of Genesis reveals that we have been created in the image and likeness of God. Although sin has distorted that image, the saving work of Jesus Christ restores it.

Made in God's Image

The first Creation account in Genesis tells of God's creative work through six days. Biblical scholars believe this beautiful, poetic story was originally a liturgical song. In it God creates human beings on the sixth day, after the whole world has been prepared. Because only people are made in God's own image, we are God's crowning achievement. We are "*the summit* of the Creator's work"[6] (*CCC*, 343). Pope John Paul II said this about the dignity and prominence of human beings in this story of Creation: "On the previous days, marking as it were the rhythm of the birth of the cosmos, Yahweh had created the universe. Finally he created the human being, the noblest fruit of his design" ("Letter of His Holiness Pope John Paul II to Artists," 1). Throughout the narrative, God describes each part of creation as "good." It is truly fitting that on this sixth day only, God looks at "everything he had made, and he found it very good" (Genesis 1:31).

Jesus: Restoring What Was Lost

The third chapter of the Book of Genesis contains the story known as the Fall, in which the first man and woman sin by disobeying God. Because of their choice, our likeness to God has been disfigured or distorted. The image of God is no longer clear in us. Jesus, as the perfect man, restores this image—he gives us back what had been lost by sin. "It is in Christ, Redeemer and

Reflecting God's Goodness

Because we are made in the image and likeness of the Divine Creator, our creative activity in the world can reflect God's goodness. Although we are often unconscious collaborators with God's will, we can also deliberately enter into the divine plan by our actions, our prayers, and even our suffering. By doing this we can become God's coworkers for his Kingdom (see CCC, 307).

In his "Letter of His Holiness Pope John Paul II to Artists," issued on Easter Sunday of 1999, Pope John Paul II draws particular attention to how artists reflect and embody God's creative love. He writes of the "vocation and mission" of poets, writers, sculptors, architects, musicians, actors, painters, playwrights, and filmmakers. Addressing these individuals directly, the Pope writes:

> None can sense more deeply than you artists, ingenious creators of beauty that you are, something of the pathos with which God at the dawn of creation looked upon the work of his hands. A glimmer of that feeling has shone so often in your eyes when—like the artists of every age—captivated by the hidden power of sounds and words, colours and shapes, you have admired the work of your inspiration, sensing in it some echo of the mystery of creation with which God, the sole creator of all things, has wished in some way to associate you. (1)

Do you have an artistic gift in writing, music, visual art, dance, drama, or film? How can you use that creative gift to glorify God, the Creator and Source of all that is?

Savior, that the divine image . . . has been restored to its original beauty and ennobled by the grace of God"[7] (*CCC,* 1701). Because Jesus is the "image of the invisible God" (Colossians 1:15), we are "inwardly renewed" (*The Church in the Modern World,* 22) when we become like him. In this way Jesus is truly the firstborn of a multitude of brothers and sisters united in him. ✝

Article 47 Women and Men: Partners in God's Plan

From the beginning God willed the creation of humanity as male and female (see Genesis 1:27). In creating men and women as equal partners in his plan of salvation, God has given us the gift of sexuality and has affirmed that we are not meant to be alone in the world.

Created for Each Other

Human beings were created to be in loving relationships with each other. In the Book of Genesis, when God fashions the first person (in Hebrew, *adam*) from the clay of the ground, God declares: "It is not good for the man to be alone. I will make a suitable partner for him" (2:18). After creating wild animals, birds, and cattle, God finally brings forth another person, whom Adam welcomes as "bone of my bones / and flesh of my flesh" (2:23). The *Catechism* describes the resultant partnership between man and woman as "the first form of communion between persons" (*Gaudium et spes* 12 § 4) (383).

Catholic Wisdom

Church Art

One of the purposes of the artwork in churches is to teach us about religious truths. A good example is paintings by Michelangelo in the Vatican Sistine Chapel. On the ceiling are several scenes from the Book of Genesis. You have probably seen photos or copies of the central panel, which is called "The Creation of Adam." It shows both the power of God and the dignity and beauty that God gives to humanity.

Created as Equals

God created men and women "in perfect equality as human persons"; both "possess an inalienable dignity which comes to them immediately from God their Creator" (*CCC*, 369). As creatures made in God's image, we "reflect the Creator's wisdom and goodness"[8] (369). Thus, even though men and women are physically different, we are the same in the ways that matter most. We are equal in our dignity, in our rights, and in our capacity to be signs of God's presence in the world.

Historically, the dignity and rights of women have not been universally respected. Many ongoing social problems show that this is true. For example, women and girls are often the victims of violence and especially of sexual violence. Many girls in developing countries also lack access to education. The Second Vatican Council took note of this more than forty years ago: "It is deeply to be deplored that these basic personal rights are not yet being respected everywhere, as is the case with women who are denied the chance freely to choose a husband, or a state of life, or to have access to the same educational and cultural benefits as are available to men" (*The Church in the Modern World,* 29). The Council urged our support of efforts to promote social justice, equity, and human dignity so that all God's people, both women and men, might flourish.

Created with the Gift of Sexuality

In creating us male and female, God has given us the wonderful gift of sexuality. Our sexuality is rooted in a physical body, making us either male or female. This prepares us for the possibility of marriage and family life. If God calls us to Marriage, we will join our body with that of our future spouse. If God wills it, we will then bring forth new life. However, sexuality is broader than just our physical capacity for **procreation.** "*Sexuality* affects all aspects of the human person.   It especially concerns affectivity, the capacity to love and to procreate, and in a more general way the aptitude for forming bonds of communion with others" (*CCC,* 2332). Our sexuality is a sign of our call to love and to live in communion with God and others.

The gift of sexuality comes with the responsibility to cultivate the virtue of **chastity.** To be chaste means to live a life of sexual integrity. This is easier to understand when we

procreation
Conceiving and bearing children.

chastity
The virtue by which people are able to successfully and healthfully integrate their sexuality into their total person; recognized as one of the fruits of the Holy Spirit.

Models of Cooperation in Sacred Scripture and in Church History

The Bible and Church history offer us many examples of men and women cooperating with each other and with God in the divine plan of salvation history.

In the Old Testament:

- Moses was assisted by his brother, Aaron, and his sister, Miriam, in leading the Israelites to freedom.
- Joshua leads the Israelites into the Promised Land with the valuable assistance of a woman named Rahab, who hides the Israelite spies in her home and protects them from danger.

In the New Testament:

- Mary and Joseph cooperate as spouses in raising the child Jesus.
- Jesus' disciples are both male and female. Although those identified in the Gospels as the Twelve Apostles are male, Jesus has female companions as well, such as Mary Magdalene, Joanna, and Susanna.

In Church History:

- Saint Francis and Saint Clare of Assisi were coworkers in serving the thirteenth-century Church. They founded the Franciscans and the Poor Clares, respectively.
- Dorothy Day and Peter Maurin cofounded the Catholic Worker movement in New York City in 1933. Members commit themselves to taking care of the basic material needs of the poor and advocating for social change.

Men and women laboring side by side for the glory of God—what a beautiful image of the communion that lies at the heart of the Blessed Trinity.

recognize that integrity comes from the root word *integer,* meaning "whole." To be chaste is to be whole. We must integrate our sexuality within our whole selves so that what we do with our bodies is united with the spiritual dimension of our selves. A chaste person's thoughts, words, and actions all reflect God's purpose for the gift of sexuality. All the baptized are called to develop the virtue of chastity in a way that is in keeping with their states of life. ✝

genocide

The systematic and planned extermination of an entire national, racial, or ethnic group.

embryo

The unborn child from the time it implants in the uterine wall through the eighth week of its development.

fetus

The unborn child from the end of the eighth week after conception to the moment of birth.

Article 48 Respect for Human Life

Jesus reveals that all people have inherent dignity. Therefore we must respect human life in all its forms. Catholics call this reverence for and protection of human life the "consistent ethic of life." This ethic applies to life in all its stages—at its very beginning, at its very end, and at every point in between.

The Sacred Gift of Life

Catholics understand life to be a sacred gift because "the human person has been willed for its own sake in the image and likeness of the living and holy God" (*CCC,* 2319). God is the author of all life, so only God can decide the time for an individual human life to end. Any attempt to alter this course of events is a violation of the Fifth Commandment, "You shall not kill" (Exodus 20:13). Killing another person, at any stage of that person's life, is an offense against her or his dignity and against the holiness of the Creator.

Many issues are a part of the Church's consistent ethic of life. Vatican II's *The Church in the Modern World* lists ways this ethic may be violated. They include **genocide,** suicide, torture, human trafficking, and degrading working conditions (see 27). Let's look at two sets of life issues—those that occur at life's very beginning and those that occur at life's very end.

At Life's Beginning

Human life begins at the moment of conception—when the egg and the sperm unite and a baby, a new being with a unique genetic code, begins the long process of development in the womb. For this reason the Church strongly opposes abortion—the intentional termination of a pregnancy—in all circumstances. Abortion ends the life of the most vulnerable individual in society, the developing child in its mother's womb.

Because a human **embryo** or **fetus** is a human being, created in God's image and likeness, it must be respected and protected from the moment of conception. From the first moment of existence, a human being has the rights of a person, including the right to life. Medical science has advanced to such an extent that many diseases can be diagnosed, and some even treated, while the embryo or fetus remains in the womb. Doctors can even operate on an embryo or fetus. Such procedures are acceptable if they respect the integrity and life of the embryo. They must not involve "disproportionate risks" (*CCC*, 2275) to the developing child, and they must be "directed toward its healing, the improvement of its condition of health, or its individual survival"[9] (2275).

At Life's End

Euthanasia is a direct action, or deliberate and purposeful lack of action, that causes the death of a person who is disabled, sick, or dying. The most common justification given for euthanasia is that it relieves pain and suffering by hastening death.

We act on our respect for the sanctity of life by treating those who are at the end of life with dignity, care, and compassion.

Catholic Church teaching recognizes the reality of suffering for those at the end of life, but it definitively rejects the perspective that hastening death can ever be moral. Instead we must guide dying people to see a great truth in their final days. They are deeply united with the sufferings of the Crucified Christ. We must also minimize their physical discomfort through painkillers and other medicines. What we must never do is determine the day or the hour when their earthly journey will be complete. That is God's decision to make. ✝

Part Review

1. What three basic truths are at the heart of human dignity?

2. God created humans good, so why do we need redemption?

3. What is significant in that a person is "not just something, but someone"?

4. Describe how Jesus respected the dignity of others during his earthly ministry.

5. How does Jesus restore what was lost through sin?

6. How can we participate in God's creative work?

7. Describe an example from the Bible of individuals cooperating with one another and with God in the divine plan of salvation.

8. Even though men and women are physically different, how are they created equal?

9. What is the consistent ethic of life?

10. Define *abortion* and *euthanasia* and explain why they are wrong.

Part 3

We Are Children of God

Through his saving work on earth, Jesus enables us to become adopted children of his Divine Father. In the life-giving waters of Baptism, we are transformed into this new creation through the power of the Holy Spirit. Thus, we are able to build our lives on the certain knowledge that God desires our happiness. While we live on earth, God listens attentively to our prayer, responding to us with abundant love, mercy, and compassion. God also gives us sanctifying grace so we can live in a way that reflects our Christian dignity. When our earthly life ends, God offers us a new life in Heaven: perfect and unending joy in the holy presence of the Blessed Trinity. How fortunate and blessed we are to share, both on earth and in Heaven, in God's own divine life, a life that overflows with bountiful, compassionate love for all creation.

The topics covered is this part are:

^{Article}49 God Desires Our Happiness

Everyone wants to be happy, right? But have you ever wondered if God wants you to be happy? If so, you can rest assured that the answer is yes: God created us to be truly and deeply happy, both during our time on earth and eternally in Heaven. The *Catechism* states that our desire for happiness is "of divine origin," for "God has placed it in the human heart" (1718). Because God is the source of this desire, God can truly fulfill it.

Original Blessing: Lost by Sin, Restored by Christ

The Book of Genesis offers us a vision of the happy state in which God has always desired us to live. The first people lived in harmony with God, with one another, and with nature in "an original 'state of holiness and justice'"[10] (*CCC,* 375). This original, blessed state of unity and peace was lost by human sinfulness in an event called the Fall.

Because of the Fall, humanity is in need of redemption. This means we need God to restore our ability to live in right relationship with one another and to give us again the happiness that results from living as God desires. To accomplish this, God the Father sent Jesus the Eternal Son to redeem and save us through his life, death, and Resurrection. Like the suffering servant of whom the prophet Isaiah wrote, Jesus "surrendered himself to death / and was counted among the wicked" to "take away the sins of many" (Isaiah 53:12). Or, as Saint Paul described it, Jesus "died for our sins in accordance with the scriptures" (1 Corinthians 15:3). Although he was the Perfect and Eternal Son of God, Jesus lived and died as one of us. He gave his life "as a ransom for many" (Matthew 20:28), dying for all people "without exception" (*CCC,* 605). Truly, this saving work gives us cause for happiness, gratitude, and joy.

True Joy

Believing in the saving, redemptive work of Jesus Christ does not mean we are happy every single day. Like all people, we experience good days and bad days, happiness and sorrow,

The Beatitudes

The Beatitudes present us with a specific vision of the happiness God desires for us. They are found in the Gospel of Matthew (see 5:2–10) as part of the Sermon on the Mount, a collection of many of Jesus' key teachings. In the Beatitudes Jesus proclaims certain groups of people to be blessed, such as those who mourn, the meek, the poor in spirit, the merciful, the clean of heart, and the persecuted.

These characteristics may seem like an odd description of happiness. Indeed the vision of the Kingdom that Jesus offers in the Beatitudes turns our understanding of happiness upside down. Like the prayer of Mary of Nazareth, which praises God as the One who fills the hungry and sends the rich away (see Luke 1:53), the Beatitudes tell us that happiness does not lie in money, possessions, power, or prestige. The joy that is characteristic of Christian life comes instead from showing mercy, hungering for righteousness, and making peace.

success and suffering. Yet we can find comfort and reassurance in the promise Jesus offered his disciples shortly before his death. "I have told you this so that my joy might be in you and your joy might be complete" (John 15:11). Indeed, joy is one of the fruits of the Holy Spirit, one of the "perfections that the Holy Spirit forms in us as the first fruits of eternal glory" (*CCC*, 1832). True joy is the mark of the Christian. In fact, Saint Paul urges us: "Rejoice in the Lord always. I shall say it again: rejoice!" (Philippians 4:4). Despite the inevitable ups and downs of daily life, faith in Jesus offers us a rock-solid foundation on which to build a life that offers us deep and abiding joy. ☩

Catholic Wisdom

Made for Happiness

What do we need to be truly happy? Pope John Paul II spoke about this at the World Youth Day welcoming ceremony in 2002. He points us to where we can find the answer: *"People are made for happiness. Rightly, then, you thirst for happiness. Christ has the answer to this desire of yours. But he asks you to trust him. True joy is a victory, something which cannot be obtained without a long and difficult struggle. Christ holds the secret of this victory"* ("17th World Youth Day, Papal Welcoming Ceremony, Address by the Holy Father John Paul II, July 25, 2002," 2).

50 Baptism: Becoming God's Adopted Children

The saving work of Jesus Christ on earth reveals that we are able to become children of God. This happens through the Sacrament of Baptism, in which we receive sanctifying grace and come to share in the life of the Blessed Trinity.

Children and Heirs

Baptism gives us a whole new relationship with God. We become God's freely adopted children and heirs of God's promises. As the *Catechism* describes it, this Sacrament transforms the newly baptized person into "'a new creature' . . . who has become a 'partaker of the divine nature,'[11] member of Christ and co-heir with him,[12] and a temple of the Holy Spirit"[13] (1265). Saint Paul contrasts the new status of the baptized person—a freely adopted son or daughter of God—with his or her former state—a slave to sin. In his Letter to the Romans, he writes:

> For those who are led by the Spirit of God are children of God. For you did not receive a spirit of slavery to fall back into fear, but you received a spirit of adoption, through which we cry "*Abba,* Father!" The Spirit itself bears witness with our spirit that we are children of God, and if children, then heirs, heirs of God and joint heirs with Christ, if only we suffer with him so that we may also be glorified with him. (8:14–17)

Saint Paul expressed a similar idea in his letter to the Galatians: "You are no longer a slave but a child, and if a child then also an heir, through God. (4:7)

Baptism also gives us a whole new relationship with other believers. Because all baptized people have become God's adopted children, the differences among people that may seem important in other parts of life are not important in the Church. Baptism creates profound equality among believers, for through it we are reborn as "the one People of God of the New Covenant, which transcends all the natural or human limits of nations, cultures, races, and sexes" (*CCC,* 1267). Saint Paul describes this reality in a Scripture passage used in the baptismal liturgies of the early Church: "Through faith you are all children of God in Christ Jesus. For all of you who were baptized into Christ have clothed

The Liturgy of Baptism

Have you ever been to a liturgy at which a Baptism was celebrated? The rituals, signs, and symbols of this Sacrament make clear how it transforms us into a new and grace-filled creation.

- **Water.** Immersion in water indicates that Baptism is our rebirth in the Spirit. When we are plunged into the waters of the font, we die with Christ. When we rise up from those waters, we rise to a new life in him.
- **Oil.** Anointing with Sacred Chrism (perfumed oil) symbolizes our new mission as Christians, for we are anointed in the power of the Spirit to be "for ever a member of Christ who is Priest, Prophet, and King" (*The Rite of Baptism,* 62).
- **Light.** Lighting the baptismal candle from the Paschal (Easter) candle proclaims that we have become, like Christ, the light of the world.
- **White garment.** Putting on a white garment represents, quite literally, putting on a new identity as a Christian. The Rite of Baptism states: "You have become a new creation, and have clothed yourselves in Christ. See in this white garment the outward sign of your Christian dignity" (63).

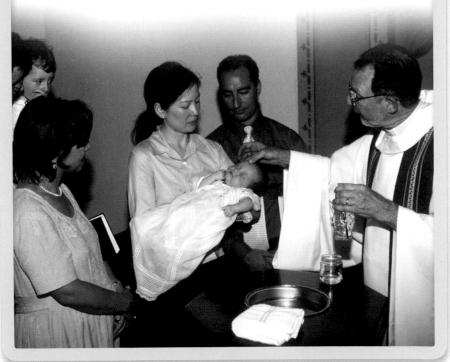

yourselves with Christ. There is neither Jew nor Greek, there is neither slave nor free person, there is not male and female; for you are all one in Christ Jesus" (Galatians 3:26–28).

The Role of Grace

The **sanctifying grace** of Baptism transforms both our relationship with God and our relationship with other believers. Grace is a freely offered gift of God. It is not something we earn, work for, or deserve. The grace we receive in Baptism enables us to share in "the intimacy of the Trinitarian life" (*CCC*, 2021) and to respond wholeheartedly to our Christian vocation of living in a way that is worthy of God's adopted children. ✝

sanctifying grace
A supernatural gift of God by which our sins are forgiven, we are made holy, and our friendship with God is restored.

Article
51 Our Ultimate Destiny: Eternal Life

As God's beloved children, created in love and redeemed by grace, we are destined to live forever in the glory of his holy presence. Faith in God leads us to turn to him alone as our "first origin" and our "ultimate goal" and to neither prefer anything to him nor substitute anything for him (*CCC*, 229). In other words, we came from God, and to him we will one day return, and nothing can take his place in our lives.

Sharing in Jesus' Resurrection

After Jesus had freely submitted himself to suffering and death, God the Father raised him up to glorious new life. This event is called the Resurrection. Jesus' Resurrection is not only about him, but also about us. Do you know why? In Baptism we are baptized into Christ's death so that when we die, we may also share in his Resurrection. Saint Paul explains it this way:

> Are you unaware that we who were baptized into Christ Jesus were baptized into his death? We were indeed buried with him through baptism into death, so that, just as Christ was raised from the dead by the glory of the Father, we too might live in newness of life.
>
> For if we have grown into union with him through a death like his, we shall also be united with him in the resurrection. (Romans 6:3–5)

The Catholic Funeral Liturgy

Although funerals are sad occasions, the rituals and symbols of Catholic funerals stress our belief that all the baptized are destined to share in eternal life with God. In fact, many elements of the funeral liturgy explicitly connect with the liturgy of Baptism:

- **Holy water:** Sprinkling the coffin or urn with holy water "reminds the assembly of the saving waters of Baptism" *(Order of Christian Funerals, 36)*.

- **Funeral pall:** Covering the coffin with a white cloth, called a pall, is a sign of Christian dignity, which calls to mind "the baptismal garment of the deceased" (38).

- **Paschal candle:** The lighting of the Paschal (Easter) candle "reminds the faithful of Christ's undying presence among them, of his victory over sin and death, and of their share in that victory by virtue of their initiation" (35).

- **Incense:** Incensing the coffin or urn is "a sign of honor to the body of the deceased, which through Baptism became the temple of the Holy Spirit" (37).

Even as we grieve the loss of our loved one, we can take comfort, and even find joy, in our confident hope that he or she now shares in the glorious life of the Blessed Trinity— a life we hope, one day, to experience ourselves.

© Bill Wittman/www.wpwittman.com

To put it more simply, we who have been baptized into Christ's own body will, like him, be raised to immortality. We will live forever with God, sharing in the life of the Blessed Trinity.

Heaven

This perfect life in the presence and communion of the Blessed Trinity is, of course, **Heaven.** "Heaven is the ultimate end and fulfillment of the deepest human longings, the state of supreme, definitive happiness" (*CCC,* 1024). It is "the

blessed community of all who are perfectly incorporated into Christ" (1026). Through his death and Resurrection, Jesus made Heaven accessible to all people "who die in God's grace and friendship" (1023), who have been faithful to the divine will, and who are "perfectly purified" (1023). Some people are already perfectly purified when they die; others will experience a final cleansing in **Purgatory** before entering Heaven.

What is Heaven like? Because we will not experience Heaven until after we die, "this mystery of blessed communion with God and all who are in Christ is beyond all understanding and description" (*CCC*, 1027). Sacred Scripture conveys the beauty and joy of Heaven through symbols and images, like "light, peace, wedding feast, wine of the kingdom, the Father's house, the heavenly Jerusalem, paradise"[14] (1027). No symbol, however, can fully capture the power and awe of seeing God face to face, "as he is" (1 John 3:2).

When do we go to Heaven? Immediately upon our death, our immortal soul is judged to be worthy or unworthy of Heaven. This event is called the Particular Judgment. However, God has also revealed that there will be a "final encounter with Christ in his second coming" (*CCC*, 1021). This event, the end of the world as we have known it, is called the Final, or Last, Judgment (see Matthew 25:31–46). ✝

Heaven
A state of eternal life and union with God, in which one experiences full happiness and the satisfaction of the deepest human longings.

Purgatory
A state of final purification or cleansing, which one may need to enter following death and before entering Heaven.

© 26kot/shutterstock.com

Pray It!

Act of Hope

Are you familiar with the prayer called the "Act of Hope"? This prayer affirms that Jesus is our Redeemer and expresses our hope for eternal life:

O my God, trusting in your infinite goodness and promises, I hope to obtain pardon of my sins, the help of your grace, and life everlasting, through the merits of Jesus Christ, my Lord and redeemer. Amen.

Article 52
Bringing Our Needs to God in Prayer

As God's beloved children, we know we can confidently approach God with our needs, desires, and concerns in prayer. But sometimes prayer can be difficult. We may wonder whether God really listens to us or whether our prayers are always answered. At times like this, several Scripture passages can help us to stick it out, to persevere in our prayer despite our doubts. Let's explore what these passages can teach us about prayer.

The Friend at Midnight (Luke 11:5–8)

Jesus tells this parable, a story that uses metaphor to teach, about someone who has unexpected guests at midnight. Completely unprepared, he asks a friend to loan him three loaves of bread so he might extend hospitality to his guests and offer them a meal. Although the friend will be annoyed at being disturbed in the middle of the night, "he will get up to give him whatever he needs because of his persistence" (11:8).

Jesus uses this story to teach us that our prayer should be persistent and courageous. Like the man who boldly knocks on a door at midnight to ask for what he needs, we can be forthright with God, sharing our needs, concerns, and problems. And like the friend who responds to the one in need, we know God will always respond to our needs with merciful love.

How do you pray when you need to bring your cares and concerns to God?

Ask, Seek, Knock (Matthew 7:7–11)

Jesus continues his teaching about prayer by assuring us that if we ask, we will receive; if we seek, we will find; and if we knock, the door will be opened to us. He compares the love and fidelity of his Divine Father to the love of a human father for his children. If a human father knows how to give his children what they need, then "how much more will your heavenly Father give good things to those who ask him" (7:11)?

The Persistent Widow (Luke 18:1–8)

To understand how this parable instructs us about prayer, we must understand the vulnerable position of widows during the time of Jesus. A widow had to rely on the goodwill of her own family or her deceased husband's family to ensure her survival. Their failure to provide for her could mean the difference between life and death. The widow in this story may have been in a situation like this, for she actively seeks a "just decision" against her adversary (18:5).

The judge before whom she places her case "neither feared God nor respected any human being" (18:2). Yet because she persistently makes her request, never giving up and never backing down, she succeeds. The judge renders a verdict in her favor.

This parable teaches us about the necessity of praying always "without becoming weary" (18:1). If this corrupt and unjust judge can be persuaded to do the right thing, "will not God then secure the rights of his chosen ones who call out to him day and night? Will he be slow to answer them? I tell you, he will see to it that justice is done for them speedily" (18:7–8).

What about "Unanswered" Prayer?

All these Scripture passages teach us to be faithful and persistent in our prayer, never losing heart. What about the times when our prayers seem to go unanswered? Is God not listening? Is he just being slow in responding? Or is something else going on?

The *Catechism* states that God is not "an instrument to be used" (2735). In other words, our prayer requests are not God's "to do" list to follow as we have specified. He is indeed faithful to us, but sometimes this fidelity does not take the form we expect or desire.

When we pray it is important to focus not on our will but on God's will. God hears all our prayers; he often answers them in ways we do not see.

© Annie Griffiths Belt/CORBIS

For example, what we ask of God may not be in our best interest. Or he may have another plan for us, which gradually unfolds and becomes clear. Or he may answer our prayers in a different way than we had hoped, a way we cannot yet understand. If we follow the advice of Saint Paul and "pray without ceasing" (1 Thessalonians 5:17), we will grow in our ability to trust in God's goodness and grace. Even when our prayers seem to go unanswered, we will come to believe that God never fails to embrace us in our time of need, offering us gentle mercy and abundant compassion. ✝

Liturgy of the Hours

The Liturgy of the Hours is an ancient prayer tradition that belongs to the whole Church. It is a method of structured daily prayer focused on a four-week cycle of Scripture readings, especially the Psalms. It can be prayed alone or with others at morning, evening, or other times of the day. It can be prayed from a book called a breviary, or it can be prayed online. You can even download a podcast. Because Christians throughout the world pray the Liturgy of the Hours, we unite with the global Body of Christ even when we pray it alone.

If the Liturgy of the Hours sounds appealing to you, ask your teacher or campus minister to help you find some printed or online resources.

Live It!

Nagging God

Did you ever think that nagging could get you somewhere with God? Nagging is certainly not valued in our friendships or family relationships. But in Luke 11: 5–13, Jesus advises us to nag God for the things we really need. Of course, what we nag for makes the difference. So don't ever give up on God. Be persistent in praying for your needs and the needs of others.

Part Review

1. Where does the human desire for happiness come from?

2. What do the Beatitudes tell us about happiness?

3. What are the effects of the Sacrament of Baptism?

4. What is sanctifying grace?

5. In what way is Jesus' Resurrection also about us?

6. What is Heaven?

7. Explain how the rituals and symbols of a Catholic funeral connect with the liturgy of Baptism.

8. Why might our prayers seem to go unanswered at times?

Part 4

Jesus Reveals Our Call to Holiness

One of the best ways to learn about Jesus' teachings is to read the Gospels. Though all four Gospels, in their entirety, are worthy of our prayerful reflection, certain passages make our call to holiness especially clear. In passages like the Sermon on the Mount, Jesus' conversation with the rich man, the Great Commandment, and the parables, we learn what Jesus asks of those who have made the commitment to be his disciples. We glimpse the vision of the Reign of God, in which Jesus invites us to share. We gain an understanding of how our choice to be faithful to Jesus' teachings is a participation in God's Reign on earth. We receive strength for our journey toward our ultimate destiny—union with the life of the Blessed Trinity.

The topics covered is this part are:

^{Article}53 The Sermon on the Mount

The Sermon on the Mount is a collection of Jesus' teachings on many important topics, which the Gospel of Matthew presents as a speech given by Jesus. In it Jesus speaks about love of enemies, anger, adultery, divorce, retaliation, judging others, and prayer, among other things. This article considers several key points of this sermon.

Our Call to Beatitude

The Sermon on the Mount begins with the **Beatitudes.** These are a series of teachings in which Jesus pronounces as "blessed" certain unlikely groups of people, like the poor in spirit, the meek, and the persecuted. In this way the Beatitudes identify the actions and attitudes that are characteristic of the Christian life (see *CCC,* 1717). They also reveal that we are all called to a state of beatitude, or blessing, as "the goal of human existence, the ultimate end of human acts" (1719). This state of beatitude—also called the Kingdom or Reign of God, the vision of God, the joy of the Lord, or God's rest (see 1720)—"makes us 'partakers of the divine nature' and of eternal life"[15] (1721). It enables us to share in the glory of Christ and in the joy of the Trinitarian life. This is a great gift that God freely offers to us in love.

We know that our ultimate end is sharing in the life of the Blessed Trinity. This fact invites us to conduct our lives in a way that is worthy of this destiny. The Beatitudes encourage us to put aside our desire for riches, fame, power, or prestige and to instead make mercy, peacemaking, and righteousness our priorities. In this way we enter into the blessings of the Kingdom of Heaven, which we experience now in an incomplete way while looking forward to their fullness at the end of time.

Trusting in God, Not Money

Where do you put most of your trust? In yourself? in other people? in what you have? in God? Later in the Sermon on the Mount (see Matthew 6:25–34), Jesus challenges us to put our trust in God with our whole hearts. He talks about how people worry about what they will eat or drink, about

Beatitudes

The teachings of Jesus during the Sermon on the Mount in which he describes the actions and attitudes that should characterize Christians and by which one can discover genuine meaning and happiness.

Prayer, Fasting, and Almsgiving

A portion of the Sermon on the Mount (see Matthew 6:1–6,16–18) is always read on Ash Wednesday, the beginning of the liturgical season of Lent. This passage teaches us about the traditional Lenten disciplines, or practices.

- **Prayer:** Jesus urges us to pray sincerely, seeking God's presence with humility. We are not to pray in a way that tries to draw the approval of others.
- **Fasting:** Jesus invites us to fast as an act of genuine repentance, not as a ploy to impress other people.
- **Almsgiving:** Jesus wants us to share generously with our sisters and brothers in need. We should act out of an authentic desire to lessen their suffering. We are not to seek out reward or recognition for ourselves.

Prayer, fasting, and almsgiving are interrelated practices. Prayer strengthens our resolve to fast and our generosity in giving alms. Fasting turns our hearts toward God, the Source of all we need, and cultivates compassion in us for those who will benefit from our almsgiving. Almsgiving ensures that our prayer and fasting give rise to a concrete response to the needs of the poor. Together these practices are hallmarks of Christian spirituality, both during the season of Lent and throughout the year.

© Bill Wittman/www.wpwittman.com

what they will wear, and about their physical health and appearance. Isn't it amazing that these same concerns still preoccupy people today, two thousand years after Jesus spoke those words? Jesus invites us to let go of these worries, making faith in the One he called **_Abba_** our first priority.

God alone knows what we truly need, and God alone will provide for us.

Jesus also recognizes that when we are worried, we tend to place our trust where it does not belong: in money or in material possessions. Jesus cautions against this. He reminds us that "treasures on earth" can be destroyed or stolen, whereas "treasures in heaven" last eternally (Matthew 6:19, 20). Even more significant, trusting in material things can distort our perspective regarding what is really important. We can start to value things more than people, status more than service, and money more than God. Jesus confronts us with a clear choice: we cannot serve two masters (see 6:24), so we must make a choice between God and wealth. If we choose God, we will find true and lasting joy; if we choose money, we will find only a fleeting, temporary happiness. ✝

Abba

A way of addressing God the Father used by Jesus to call attention to his—and our—intimate relationship with his Heavenly Father. *Abba* means "my Father" or "our Father" in Aramaic.

Article 54 The Parables of Jesus

Parables are stories that use metaphors based in daily life to convey religious truths. Jesus' parables are an important part of his proclamation of the Kingdom and of his invitation to all people to enter that Kingdom. As a great teacher, Jesus knew the power of a vivid story to captivate the imagination and win the hearts of his listeners. Although the parables are not long (the shortest is just one verse; the longest is twenty-one verses), they are memorable, powerful, and thought provoking. They often contain a twist, or some element of surprise, that shocks us into thinking differently about ourselves, the world, or God. They force us to confront ourselves, to examine our priorities, and to make difficult

Catholic Wisdom

Pope Benedict XVI on Parables

In his book *Jesus of Nazareth* (Doubleday, 2007), Pope Benedict XVI devotes a chapter to the message of the parables. He explores the nature and purpose of the parables and discusses the Parable of the Good Samaritan, the Parable of the Lost Son, and the Parable of the Rich Man and Lazarus. Look for the book in your school library and learn more about Jesus' messages to us through the parables.

choices. Through them, Jesus calls us to take our places at the feast of the Kingdom.

This article considers several of the more than thirty parables of Jesus contained in the Gospels.

The Treasure in the Field and the Pearl of Great Price (Matthew 13:44–46)

These parables are among the shortest Jesus tells—two of them in a mere three verses. In both, a person sells everything he has to buy only one thing. In the first parable, that one thing is a field in which he has found a treasure; in the second parable, it is a fine, valuable pearl. These stories invite us to commit ourselves fully to our lives of discipleship, responding wholeheartedly to Jesus' proclamation of the Kingdom. This level of commitment certainly carries a great cost and involves sacrifice on our part. However, notice the attitude of the man in the first parable. He sells all he has "out of joy" (verse 44). When we are open to the presence and grace of the Holy Spirit, making a sacrifice for the sake of the Kingdom need not be burdensome. It can, in fact, be a delight.

The Great Feast (Luke 14:16–24)

In Luke's Gospel, Jesus tells a parable about a man who hosts a dinner party. The invited guests all give reasons why they cannot attend the event. Although their excuses seem reasonable (for example, they have just made a major purchase, or they have just gotten married), the host is angered. In deciding to fill his home with the poor, the crippled, the blind, and the lame, the host offers us an image of the Kingdom of Heaven—a great banquet at which all are welcome, perhaps especially those who are not welcome anywhere else. This parable invites us to think about how our actions and decisions—especially our decisions to include or exclude others—reflect this vision of the Kingdom.

The Parables of Luke, Chapter 15

Chapter 15 of Luke's Gospel contains three of the best known and best-loved parables of Jesus, all of which express a common theme. In the first parable, a sheep is lost, and the shepherd leaves his ninety-nine other sheep in the desert so he can search for the one lost sheep. When he finds it, he invites his friends and neighbors to rejoice with him. The second parable is similarly structured: a woman who has lost one of her ten coins diligently searches her home until she finds it. Like the shepherd, she also calls her friends to celebrate with her when she finds it.

In the third and final parable in this sequence, a son is lost, not so much physically as emotionally and spiritually. When he finally makes his way back home, his father runs to greet him, welcomes him with joy, and throws him a party.

These parables tell us much about the Kingdom Jesus preached. If we imagine ourselves as the lost sheep, the lost coin, or the lost son, these stories show us that no matter how long we have been lost in sin or how far away we have strayed, it is never too late to turn our hearts back toward God. If we imagine God as the shepherd searching for his sheep, as the woman hunting for her coin, or as the father waiting for his son, we see a God of infinite mercy whose patience never runs out and whose love will never fail to find us, welcome us home, and rejoice at our return. ☩

Read Luke 15:11–32. Whom in the parable can you identify with? When in your life have you felt lost, like the younger son? abandoned like the father? jealous like the older son?

synoptic Gospels

The Gospels of Mark, Matthew, and Luke are called *synoptic*—a word meaning "seen together"—because they appear to have been written using similar sources.

Article 55 Jesus and the Rich Man (Mark 10:17–22)

In the Gospels, Jesus tells us what we must do to grow in holiness and in goodness. Although he invites us to commit our lives to serving him by serving our sisters and brothers in need, many of us may find that other priorities can stand in our way, interfering with our wholehearted commitment to Christian discipleship. For those of us who find that a love of money or an attachment to material possessions stands in our way, Jesus' words to the rich man challenge us to rethink our priorities. Although there are parallel passages in the other **synoptic Gospels,** this article focuses on the one-on-one conversation Jesus has with a rich man in Mark's Gospel.

"Good Teacher, What Must I Do?"

When the rich man asks what he must do to inherit eternal life, Jesus responds by quoting a shortened version of the Ten Commandments, laws that would have been very familiar to a faithful Jew. When the man indicates that he has observed these laws since the days of his youth, Jesus looks at him with love. Why does Jesus love this person? He does not seem to have done anything particularly extraordinary or heroic, yet Jesus recognizes in the man a sincere desire to follow him. This man has sought out Jesus, making an effort to ask this question and to listen to Jesus' response. Although the man has been living in a way that is pleasing to God all his life, he desires to do more.

Pray It!

When Jesus Calls

Dear Jesus, help us not to be afraid of your call, whether in small or big things. Sometimes we can get comfortable and think we are doing enough in response. Sometimes we get too concerned about what others will think about us. When these things happen, help us to be fearless and to strive to do more.

Jesus, help us to be open in our prayer to hear your call. Open our ears to your Word so we can better live its meaning in our daily lives. Give us the grace we need to become more like you. Amen.

"Go, Sell What You Have"

Jesus recognizes that this man's possessions and wealth stand in the way of his further growth in holiness. Jesus asks the man to sell what he has and to give to the poor. He invites the man to a life that is focused not on acquiring more possessions but on caring for all those in need. Jesus asks the man to live in a way that witnesses to the power and presence of the Kingdom of Heaven on earth.

Dorothy Day of New York

Dorothy Day was born in 1897 in Brooklyn, New York, and made her career as a journalist. Baptized Episcopalian, she did not practice her faith until she became pregnant outside of marriage and decided to have her daughter baptized as a Catholic. She herself soon followed suit, becoming Catholic in 1927. When she met the activist Peter Maurin several years later, the two started an organization called the Catholic Worker. They published a newspaper that advocated for the rights of workers and opened a "house of hospitality" to provide food, shelter, and other assistance to the many people in New York struggling during the Great Depression.

The Catholic Worker soon grew into a nationwide, and then worldwide, movement. Today, houses of hospitality continue the work Day and Maurin began by serving the poor in the name of Christ and by advocating for just social policies.

Dorothy Day died on November 29, 1980. She had truly lived out the words of Jesus to the rich man: "Sell what you have, and give to the poor" (Mark 10:21). She challenges each of us to examine our own willingness to make service of the poor and the transformation of unjust social structures priorities in our lives.

The man has no further response to Jesus' instructions: "His face fell, and he went away sad, for he had many possessions" (Mark 10:22). The story ends here. We don't know if the man accepted Jesus' invitation or not. Was he able to overcome his sadness? Or was he too afraid to let go of his many possessions, too scared to shift the priorities in his life? We can only speculate about the answers to these questions about the rich man. However, we can ask some difficult questions of ourselves: How important are material possessions in our lives? Are we willing to live with less in order to help our neighbors who are in great need? Are we willing to serve Christ, who was materially poor during his earthly life, by serving the poor in our world today? ✝

Article 56 The Greatest Commandments (Matthew 22:34–40)

In Matthew's Gospel, a Pharisee asks Jesus which commandment in the Jewish Law is the greatest, or most important. Jesus responds with two answers. First, he quotes from the Book of Deuteronomy: "You shall love the LORD, your God, with all your heart, and with all your soul, and with all your strength" (6:5). Then he quotes from the Book of Leviticus: "You shall love your neighbor as yourself" (19:18).

This seems simple, right? Jesus has managed to summarize the whole Jewish tradition of the "law and the prophets" (Matthew 22:40), as well as the whole message of the Gospel, in just two short sentences. Yet questions remain for us: How exactly are we to love God? How are we to love our neighbor? The Ten Commandments (see Exodus 20:1–17) provide some insight into the specifics of how we are to live out the Great Commandment of love.

How Do We Love God?

The first three Commandments focus on how we are to love God.

- "The first commandment embraces faith, hope, and charity"[16] (*CCC,* 2086). It invites us to believe and hope in God, loving God above all else. We live this Commandment when we worship and pray faithfully, resisting the tempta-

tion to make other things—like power, pleasure, or possessions—more important than God.

- The Second Commandment echoes the words of Psalm 8:
"O LORD, our Lord, / how awesome is your name through
all the earth!" (verse 2). We are to speak God's name only
in reverence, love, and respect, never using it in a way that
expresses hatred, dishonesty, or violence.

- As the day on which the Lord Jesus rose from the dead,
Sunday is the holiest day of the Christian week. God asks us
to respect the sacredness of this day by participating in the
celebration of the Eucharist, resting from our usual business
of work or school, and enjoying the company of our family
and friends.

How Do We Love Our Neighbor?

Commandments four through ten focus on how we are to
love our neighbor:

- God wills that we honor our parents, to whom we owe our
lives, with "respect, gratitude, just obedience, and assistance" (CCC, 2251). Parents, likewise, are to love their children by providing them with a safe, nurturing home and by
educating them in the Christian faith.

- All human life, at every stage of its development, is sacred
"because the human person has been willed for its own
sake in the image and likeness of the living and holy God"
(CCC, 2319). For this reason we must never participate in
the intentional taking of an innocent human life, whether
through abortion, euthanasia, suicide, or war. We can,
however, defend ourselves and others against an "unjust
aggressor" (CCC, 2321) by rendering that person unable to
harm us.

- God asks that we respect the gift of our sexuality, delight-
ing in our identity and dignity as male or female. Intimate
sexual activity must occur only within the context of a marriage relationship.

- Our parents and other adults have taught us, from a very
young age, to respect the property of others and not to take
what does not belong to us. However, we also must recognize the demand of charity and justice: to share our goods
and property generously with others. Failure to do so is a
form of theft from those who are hungry or poor.

- We are called to speak and act truthfully, never deceiving others or ruining their reputations by spreading lies, rumors, and gossip.
- God invites us to be pure in our hearts, bodies, and minds, recognizing the human body—both our own and that of others—"as a temple of the Holy Spirit, a manifestation of divine beauty" (*CCC*, 2519).
- God asks that we resist greed, envy, and the desire for wealth and material possessions. Instead, we must cultivate good will toward our neighbors, a spirit of humility, and a sense of trust that God will never fail to provide all we need. ✝

The Ten Commandments (Exodus 20:1–17)

1. I am the LORD your God: you shall not have strange gods before me.
2. You shall not take the name of the LORD, your God, in vain.
3. Remember to keep holy the LORD's Day.
4. Honor your father and mother.
5. You shall not kill.
6. You shall not commit adultery.
7. You shall not steal.
8. You shall not bear false witness against your neighbor.
9. You shall not covet your neighbor's wife.
10. You shall not covet your neighbor's goods.

57 The Last Judgment (Matthew 25:31–46)

Parousia

The second coming of Christ, when his Kingdom will be fully established and his triumph over evil will be complete.

Jesus makes the poor a priority in his teaching, healing, and proclamation of the Kingdom. From the very beginning of his public ministry, when he announces that he has been sent to "bring glad tidings to the poor" (Luke 4:18), to his declaration that the Kingdom itself belongs to the poor (see 6:20), Jesus invites his followers to a new awareness of, and response to, the plight of those oppressed by poverty. In his teaching about the Last Judgment (see Matthew 25:31–46), Jesus makes clear that we must actively love the poor if we want to enter his Kingdom.

The Parable of the Sheep and the Goats

Jesus' teaching about the Last Judgment is centered on a parable about a shepherd separating his sheep from his goats. The deeper meaning of the story quickly becomes clear: it describes the **Parousia,** and it reveals the criteria by which all people will one day be judged. In it the "sheep" are invited into the Kingdom of the Divine Father. They have consistently responded to the needs of the suffering by offering food, drink, clothing, hospitality, care, and companionship. In contrast, the "goats" are sent "into the eternal fire prepared for the devil and his angels" (Matthew 25:41) because they have failed to respond to the hungry, the poor, the sick, and the imprisoned. The surprise of this story

Live It!

Corporal Works of Mercy

How you can live the corporal works of mercy in your life? You might think, "I don't have much money, power, or experience, so what can I do?" In fact, there is a lot you can do. You can volunteer at soup kitchens, shelters, food pantries, and the like. You can give time to the sick and elderly in hospitals and nursing homes or get involved in clothing and food drives. You can help with fund-raisers to benefit people in need, from the homeless to the imprisoned. You can donate money you might have spent on going to the movies or downloading music to a charity that helps the poor. With a little creativity, you can find countless ways to live the corporal works of mercy. You can also invite your friends and family to participate with you. What is something you can do today?

lies in the presence of Jesus: he is hidden within the "least ones" (25:45), much to the shock of both the "sheep" and the "goats." He seems to have been so well concealed that the "sheep" did not realize that in serving the least, they served him, and the "goats" did not realize that in ignoring the least, they ignored him.

The Works of Mercy

The Parable of the Sheep and the Goats has given rise to the Church's teaching about the corporal and spiritual works of mercy. The *Catechism* describes the works of mercy as "charitable actions by which we come to the aid of our neighbor,"[17] attending to both "spiritual and bodily necessities"[18] (2447).

Practicing the corporal works of mercy means offering care for a person's basic physical needs:

- Feed the hungry.
- Give drink to the thirsty.
- Shelter the homeless.
- Clothe the naked.
- Care for the sick.
- Help the imprisoned.
- Bury the dead.

The spiritual works of mercy care for a person's emotional, intellectual, or spiritual needs:

- Share knowledge.
- Give advice to those who need it.
- Comfort those who suffer.
- Forgive those who hurt you.
- Correct those who need it.
- Pray for the living and the dead.

Both the corporal and spiritual works of mercy invite us to share with others the bountiful mercy God shares with us. When we share mercy with others, we stand in **solidarity** with them, knowing that we are united in our common need for God's healing love and grace.

© Bill Wittman/www.wpwittman.com

The Challenge of True Discipleship

The Parable of the Sheep and the Goats makes clear that the standard for genuine discipleship is not what we say but what we do. If we say we want to serve the poor or alleviate the suffering of the hungry and then do not follow through with concrete actions, Jesus himself will confront us with our hypocrisy.

It is significant that Jesus speaks this parable just shortly before his Passion begins. As the last parable in the Gospel of Matthew, it is among his parting words to his disciples. As he is about to undertake the saving work of his suffering and death, Jesus teaches the disciples that their lives of generous service must embody the same spirit of willing sacrifice that lies at the heart of his life and his death. ✝

solidarity
Union of one's heart and mind with all people. Solidarity leads to the just distribution of material goods, creates bonds between opposing groups and nations, and leads to the spread of spiritual goods such as friendship and prayer.

Part Review

1. What are the Beatitudes and what do they teach?

2. Identify and explain three traditional Lenten practices.

3. What is a parable?

4. What do the parables of the lost sheep, the lost coin, and the lost son tell us about the Kingdom of God?

5. What does Jesus ask the rich man to do to inherit eternal life? Why?

6. What are the Greatest Commandments?

7. What do the first three Commandments tell us about loving God?

8. At the Last Judgment, what is the standard by which all people will be judged?

9. What is the significance of Jesus' teaching the Parable of the Sheep and the Goats shortly before his Passion?

10. What are the works of mercy?

Faith and Our Response to Jesus

Part 1

What Is Faith?

Have you ever really thought about what faith is? It is not something we can touch or hold, nor is it something we can directly see or hear. We cannot design a scientific experiment to test for the presence of faith in a particular person or situation, nor can we verify which figures from history, even religious history, have acted out of a genuine faith and which have not. If faith is so difficult to pin down, what is it, exactly?

Faith is both God's gift to us and our free response to that gift. Through the theological virtue of faith, God prepares all of us to respond to his revealed truth with our whole hearts and minds. When our response is genuine and deeply rooted, truly a part of our lives, it transforms us. We seek to understand it more fully. We are moved to express it through our words and actions. We want to share it with others, hoping they will find the same peace and joy we have found in freely surrendering our whole selves to the truth God has revealed to us.

The topics covered is this part are:

58 Faith and Religion

theological virtues
The name for the God-given virtues of faith, hope, and love. These virtues make us open to living in a relationship with the Holy Trinity and are the foundation of the Christian moral life, animating it and giving it a special character.

lament
A prayer, petition, or ritual of grief that honors the death of a loved one. Many of the psalms are examples of lament recorded in the Bible.

Faith begins with God. Faith is the **theological virtue** that God gives to every person to enable us to accept God's revealed truth. Through faith we are able "to submit freely to the word that has been heard, because its truth is guaranteed by God, who is Truth itself" (*Catechism of the Catholic Church [CCC]*, 144).

Faith and Religion Are Inseparable

How is religious practice connected to faith? We might say that faith and religion are two sides of the same coin. In faith we accept God's Revelation, and we express that faith in our religious beliefs and practices. We can think of faith as the surrender of our whole selves—minds, hearts, and spirits—to God's saving love, and religion as the practices of prayer, worship, and service and the shared beliefs that result from surrendering ourselves to God's love.

Faith and religion are so closely connected that we cannot truly have one without the other. If we try to sustain our faith without expressing it through religion, it will eventually fade away. True faith is always expressed in religious worship and outreach. On the other hand, if we engage in religious practices that are not expressions of an authentic faith, we are simply going through the motions. Our religion becomes an empty ritual, a meaningless collection of words, gestures, and actions.

Religion: Worship and Adoration

When confronted with the Devil tempting him in the desert, Jesus quotes the Book of Deuteronomy: "You shall worship

Catholic Wisdom

Stars: Theological Virtues

The theological virtues—the gifts of faith, hope, and love—are essential to our lives as disciples of Christ. Pope John Paul II expressed their importance in this way: "Faith, hope and love are like three stars that rise in the sky of our spiritual life to guide us to God. They are the theological virtues *par excellence*: they put us in communion with God and lead us to him" ("General Audience," 1).

the Lord, your God, / and him alone shall you serve" (Luke 4:8). Worship of God is a key component of religion; without it we cannot say we are truly practicing our faith. Because God is the Source of all that we are, worship of God is our duty. Through worship we "render to God what we as creatures owe him in all justice" (*CCC*, 2095).

Adoration acknowledges God "as the Creator and Savior, the Lord and Master of everything that exists, as infinite

The Book of Psalms

The Book of Psalms is a beautiful resource we can use in our worship and adoration of God. It has been called the prayer book of ancient Israel, for the prayers it contains were frequently used in Temple worship. As a faithful Jew, Jesus would have prayed the Psalms regularly. Today the Psalms are commonly used in Jewish and Christian prayer. In Catholic liturgy every celebration of the Eucharist includes a psalm as part of the Liturgy of the Word. The Church's official daily prayer, the Liturgy of the Hours, is entirely built upon praying all 150 Psalms within a four-week cycle.

The Psalms are an incredibly diverse collection of prayers. They express thanksgiving, petition, **lament,** and countless other human emotions and attitudes. However, praise of God's great and constant goodness is the backdrop for all the psalms. Indeed "the prayer of the psalms is always sustained by praise" (*CCC*, 2589). In other words, even the psalms that express sadness, fear, doubt, frustration, confusion, and anger ultimately acclaim God's saving works—God's fidelity to Israel in every time and place. Consider the passages at the right from the Psalms.

"The LORD watches over the way of the just."
(1:6)

"You will show me the path to life,
abounding joy in your presence."
(16:11)

"The LORD is my light and my salvation;
whom do I fear?
The LORD is my life's refuge;
of whom am I afraid?"
(27:1)

"The LORD is good to all, compassionate to every creature."
(145:9)

The next time you are moved to praise God, to offer adoration and worship to your Creator, let these and other psalms give you the words to express your prayer.

and merciful Love" (*CCC*, 2096). In prayerful adoration, "lifting up the mind toward God" (2098), we praise the One whose goodness and mercy holds us in life, recalling that every blessing we enjoy is a gracious gift of this kind and gentle God.

Religion: Service and Sacrifice

The religious practices through which we express our faith include not only worship and adoration of God but also service and sacrifice offered on behalf of our neighbor. In other words, religion is not something we practice just in church or when we pray; rather, we practice our religion each time we share generously with those who are poor, offer assistance to our neighbors, and help our parents and other family members. In sacrificing our time, money, or other resources for the good of others, we unite ourselves more fully with the sacrifice Christ offered on the cross, making our whole lives "a sacrifice to God" (*CCC*, 2100). ✝

Article 59 Faith: A Gift from God

Faith is a supernatural gift that God freely offers to us. Through it we come to believe in and accept the truth God has revealed to us. None of us can make the decision to believe on our own; rather, it is divine grace and the help of the Holy Spirit that makes our faith possible (see *CCC*, 179).

Our "Yes" to God's Revelation

In Matthew's Gospel, Jesus confronts his disciples with the question "Who do you say that I am?" (16:15). Peter responds with a perfect confession of faith in Jesus: "You are the Messiah, the Son of the living God" (verse 16). Jesus says that "flesh and blood has not revealed this to you, but my heavenly Father" (verse 17). Jesus indicates that Peter has come to believe in something that God the Father has revealed to him—something he could not have known any other way. Through the grace of God the Father and the help of the Holy Spirit, Peter exercises the gift of faith.

We do the same thing when we willingly accept God's invitation to believe in Revelation, even when the truths of Revelation do not make perfect sense to us. The *Catechism* acknowledges that "revealed truths can seem obscure to human reason and experience" (157); yet we trust their authenticity because we trust in the One who has revealed these things to us.

Although believing the truths of Revelation is possible only with the Holy Spirit's help, doing so does not contradict our human freedom or reason. In fact, believing is a fundamentally human act. Think about it: we believe what other people—like friends, family members, or classmates—tell us, all the time. Why not also believe what God tells us? As a truly human act, our belief in God must come from our own free choice. Jesus invited—but never forced—all people to be his friends and followers during his earthly life. In the same way, he invites us to believe in and follow him today. As with any invitation, we must freely choose to accept or reject it.

The Obedience of Faith

In his Letter to the Romans, Saint Paul writes about the "obedience of faith" (1:5). The word *obedience* comes from a Latin root meaning "to hear, listen, or pay attention to." When we are obedient to God in faith, we listen carefully to God's Word and then freely surrender our whole selves—intellect, personal will, heart, and mind—to it "because its truth is guaranteed by God" (*CCC*, 144). We pay attention to Revelation, even when it seems mysterious or incomprehensible. We humbly seek God's will for our lives, eager to trust in all God has communicated to us.

© Erich Lessing/Art Resource, NY

This painting depicts Genesis 18:2–15, where Abraham and Sarah are visited by God's messengers. Who has God sent into your life to call you to deeper faith?

Faith Needs Nourishment

It is possible to lose the gift of faith if we do not attend to it, nourish it, and help it to grow. How can we strengthen and nourish our faith? We can read the Holy Scriptures regularly and prayerfully. We can engage in acts of charity and works of justice. We can seek the support of other believers. In our prayer we can also join the Apostles in asking the Lord to "increase our faith" (Luke 17:5). The God who first granted us this gracious gift will surely hear the prayer of a person longing for that gift to grow and flourish. ✝

Abraham: Our Ancestor in Faith

Abraham is our earliest ancestor in faith. Throughout his life he repeatedly trusted in the promises of God, even when those promises seemed mysterious or even impossible to fulfill.

First, Abraham answered God's call to leave his homeland and go to a new land God showed him. In return God promised to make of Abraham "a great nation" (Genesis 12:2) even though Abraham and Sarah were elderly and childless. This faithful couple held firmly to the belief that they would have descendants—after all, God had said so. In time Abraham and Sarah conceived Isaac, even though it was long past their childbearing years. Later, when God commanded Abraham to kill Isaac as a sacrifice, Abraham did not hesitate to offer to God that which was most precious to him. When God saw Abraham's devotion, he stopped him, and a ram was sacrificed instead of Isaac.

Several New Testament books, including the Letter to the Romans and the Letter to the Hebrews, praise the faith of Abraham. He is the common spiritual ancestor of Jews and Christians. As such, he has much to teach us about trusting completely in Revelation, obediently following wherever God leads.

Article 60 Examples of Faith

Have you ever become really tired and discouraged when you have been practicing or playing a game? It can help to see other people on your team pushing to go on. We can be inspired by people around us to continue on and give our best effort. In a similar way, other people can inspire and encourage us to be faithful, especially when we are discouraged and tired.

When our own faith is weak or struggling, the generations of faithful men and women who have gone before us can offer us help and encouragement. These models of faith include people from both Testaments of the Bible as well as the saints and martyrs.

Biblical Figures: The Old Testament

The Old Testament is filled with examples of people whose careful and committed response to God's Revelation, especially in difficult circumstances, can inspire our own faith.

- The faith of Ruth led her to care for her mother-in-law, Naomi, after both women had become widows. Ruth promised Naomi that "wherever you go I will go . . . your people shall be my people, and your God my God" (Ruth 1:16). They lived together in Naomi's hometown, Bethlehem, until Ruth remarried. Ruth became the great-grandmother of King David and an ancestor of Jesus.

© Brooklyn Museum/Corbis

- Hannah showed great faith in her quest to have a child. In her prayer she promised that if God gave her a son, she would "give him to the LORD for as long as he lives" (1 Samuel 1:11). When she became pregnant, she made good on her promise, and her son grew up to become the great prophet Samuel.

- Jeremiah was terrified when God asked him to become a prophet. He told God he was too young for the job and wouldn't know what to say. But, in faith, he willingly trusted in God's will and did what was asked of him, becoming one of the greatest of the prophets.

Mary Magdalene was one of the women that supported Jesus' ministry. Who are women you see in the world today who actively support the mission of Jesus?

Biblical Figures: The New Testament

The New Testament also abounds with examples of holy men and women who freely surrendered to God's Revelation, even when that surrender required great sacrifice on their part.

- "The Virgin Mary most perfectly embodies the obedience of faith" (*CCC*, 148). From her freely offered "yes" to her role in God's plan of salvation as the Mother of Jesus, to her willingness to watch her son suffer and die on the cross, to her presence among the other disciples after Jesus' Resurrection, she is truly "the purest realization of faith" (149).

- Mary Magdalene was among the women from Galilee who accompanied Jesus and the Apostles in their traveling and preaching and provided financial support for them. In all four Gospels, she is among the first of the faithful witnesses of the Resurrected Lord Jesus, who entrusts her with the mission of proclaiming that Good News to the other disciples.

- Despite Peter's famous denials during Jesus' Passion, he was nonetheless an Apostle of great faith who had earlier confessed Jesus as "the Messiah, the Son of the living God" (Matthew 16:16). In John's Gospel, Peter professes his love for the Risen Lord Jesus three times, repenting of his three earlier denials. Peter shows us that even when our faith seriously falters, God's gracious mercy heals us, enabling us to trust in Revelation once again.

Pray It!

Saintly Prayer

The saints model faith and offer us hope and inspiration when we struggle with our faith. In prayer we can reflect on the lives of the saints, read their writings, and ask them to intercede for us. Countless resources profile the saints. Spend some time looking up saints and reading about their faith journeys. A great way to start your search is to look up saints who share your name or the names of your family members.

Saints and Martyrs

The lives of the saints, some of whom were also martyrs, are
a rich resource for us as we try to live our faith authentically,
holding on to it during difficult times.

- Saint Ignatius of Loyola put all his trust in God's Revelation while resting from an injury he had sustained on the
  battlefield. After his full recovery, he gathered a group of
  companions around him. These people became the first
  members of a new religious order, the Society of Jesus, or
  Jesuits.
- Saint Catherine of Siena's faith gave her the courage to confront Pope Gregory XI after he had fled to Avignon, France.
  She urged him to return to the holy city of Rome. Perhaps
  to her great surprise, he listened to her.
- Saint Thomas More's fidelity to Revelation cost him his life.
  King Henry VIII of England executed him when he would
  not support the king in rejecting the authority of the Pope.

Stories of these and countless other holy women and
men who have gone before us show us how to live in faith.
They demonstrate how to surrender our whole selves—
minds, hearts, and spirits—to the truth God has revealed to
us. ✝

Article 61 Faith: Our Response to Revelation

Faith is a "personal adherence" (*CCC,* 176) of our whole
selves to the God who has revealed himself to us through
both words and deeds. It involves "an assent of the intellect
and will" (176). In other words, God initiates a relationship
with us through Revelation; we respond to God through
faith.

We Respond through Discipleship

When we have faith in Jesus Christ, we become his disciples,
or followers. First, this means we seek to imitate Jesus' words
and actions. We try to make his values, attitudes, and priorities our own. We try to treat people how he treated them
during his earthly life—with dignity, compassion, and love.

Second, being a disciple means we recognize and accept Jesus as the Second Person of the Blessed Trinity, the Eternal Son of God, who took on human flesh, died to liberate us from sin, and opened a path to new life for us through his Resurrection. With grateful hearts we accept the gift of grace that, through the power of the Holy Spirit, makes us adopted children of God the Father and, therefore, brothers and sisters of Jesus and of one another.

We Respond through Evangelization

All disciples of Jesus have a common vocation, rooted in our Baptism: "a vocation to holiness and to the mission of evangelizing the world" (*CCC*, 1533). To evangelize means to share our faith in Jesus Christ and the Good News of his life, death, and Resurrection. There are many ways to witness to our faith through both our words and deeds. For example, we can actively participate in the liturgical and sacramental life of the Church and invite others to do the same. We can use our talents to proclaim and to share with others what God has revealed for our salvation. We can actively engage in acts of charity and works of justice. We can try to live "in a way worthy of the gospel of Christ" (Philippians 1:27) so others may be drawn to faith through our example. ♱

Live It!

How Can You Evangelize?

How can you evangelize in your life? We each can spread the Good News through both our words and our actions:

- You can invite a friend to attend Mass with you on Sunday.
- You can volunteer with a local food bank.
- You can help out with your parish's elementary religious education program or vacation Bible school.
- You can ask your friends to say grace before lunch at school.

These are only a few ideas; there are countless other ways you can evangelize. We all have gifts and talents we can use to help spread the Good News of Jesus Christ. What are two things you can do this week to evangelize?

The Theological Virtues

A virtue is a good habit. The three theological virtues—faith; hope; and charity, or love—"relate directly to God. . . . They have the One and Triune God for their origin, motive, and object" (CCC, 1812).

Faith
enables us to believe what God has revealed and to respond to Revelation by uniting ourselves to Christ as living members of his Body, the Church. As disciples we must profess our faith with confidence, bearing witness to it in the words and actions of our daily lives.

Hope
invites us to trust in the love of God the Father, the promises of Christ, and the grace of the Holy Spirit, especially when we feel discouraged, abandoned, or disheartened. We trust that our destiny is to share in the life of the Blessed Trinity and the joy of the heavenly banquet.

Charity
asks that we follow the Greatest Commandments of love, loving God above all else and loving our neighbors as ourselves. In the words of Saint Paul, love is the most important of the theological virtues: "So faith, hope, love remain, these three; but the greatest of these is love" (1 Corinthians 13:13).

Part Review

1. Why are faith and religion inseparable?

2. What are some of the religious practices through which we can express our faith?

3. Explain how it is true that faith is both a gift from God and also rooted in human freedom.

4. How can we nourish our faith?

5. How can the generations of faithful men and women who have gone before us help us in our own faith?

6. What does it mean to be a disciple of Jesus?

7. What is evangelization?

Part 2

We Respond to God through Prayer

Think about a good friend you are especially close to. How did you first become connected with this person? How did your relationship grow into the close friendship you now enjoy?

Any good friendship takes time to develop. We must spend extended periods of time with a person to really get to know his or her personality, interests, and values. Trust must develop before we are comfortable sharing our hopes, dreams, and fears with each other.

Our relationship with God is the same. It does not develop overnight, and it does not grow without time, effort, and commitment on our part. The time we spend with God seeking to nurture that relationship is called prayer. Although Christian prayer can take many forms, it is always rooted in the example and teachings of Jesus as found in the Gospels and in the sacramental life of the Church.

The topics covered is this part are:

62 What Is Prayer?

Prayer is fundamentally a relationship—a personal, vital, and intimate connection with the living God. Throughout the whole history of salvation, prayer unfolds as a reciprocal call between God and his people. God has never stopped inviting each and every person to encounter him in prayer. God calls to us, and we respond; God calls again, and we respond more deeply and completely.

Saint John Damascene described prayer as "the raising of one's mind and heart to God or the requesting of good things from God" (*Defide orth*, 3, 24: J. P. Migne, ed., Patrologia Graeca [Paris, 1857–1866] 94, 1089C) (*CCC*, 2590). Let's consider each of these two aspects of prayer.

Raising the Mind and Heart to God

Raising our minds and hearts to God means, first, that we try to make ourselves consciously aware of God's presence with us. The reality is that God is always with us. We dwell constantly with the One who loved us into being and redeemed us in grace. But we are not always aware of that presence, because we get busy or distracted, or we just forget. When we pray we focus our minds, hearts, and spirits on God's loving presence, seeking to be drawn into greater union with the Blessed Trinity. This enables us to open ourselves more fully to the goodness and mercy of God's gracious will for our lives.

Second, raising our hearts and minds to God means we worship God as our Creator, never forgetting that we, as creatures, wholly and completely depend on him. This

Catholic Wisdom

Aspirations

One way you can increase your awareness of God's presence throughout the day is through a prayer known as an aspiration. An aspiration is a very short prayer you can pray while you are doing other things. For example, you might simply repeat throughout your day "My Lord and my God" or "Lord, have mercy." You also can make up your own aspiration. Sometimes you might just want to say "Thanks, Jesus" or "Help me, Jesus."

prayer of petition

A prayer form in which you ask God for something you need.

intercessory prayer

A prayer form in which you ask God's help for other people's needs; also called intercession.

recognition—that God is God, and we are not—is called humility. The *Catechism* describes humility as "the foundation of prayer" (2559). Humility does not mean putting ourselves down or thinking badly of ourselves; rather, it means seeing ourselves as we really are: beloved children of God who are in constant need of divine grace as we journey toward the ultimate perfection of God's Reign.

Requesting Good Things from God

Many of us ask for good things in our prayer. This type of prayer is called **prayer of petition.** We may ask God for forgiveness of our sins. We may ask, as in the Lord's Prayer, for the coming of God's Reign and for the courage and strength to do God's will. We may also pray for our other needs, for "when we share in God's saving love, we understand that *every need* can become the object of petition" (*CCC,* 2633).

When we ask God for good things on behalf of other people, we are engaging in **intercessory prayer**—interceding with God for the needs of others. We may pray for those who are sick or suffering, for those who are poor, or for those who are mourning the loss of a loved one. When we pray in this way, we must be generous in our prayer, praying not only for our own friends or family members but also for the many people throughout the world who are in great need, especially those who have no one to pray for them. ✝

We support and strengthen one another through communal prayer. What opportunities do you have for praying with others? Use one of those opportunities this week.

© Bill Wittman/www.wpwittman.com

Tips for Prayer

If you have the desire to develop your relationship with God through prayer, here are some tips to help you get started:

Who? You can pray with anyone or with no one. If you pray with family members or friends, they can support you in your spiritual life, but praying alone can also be very fulfilling.

Where? Many people find it helpful to dedicate a specific place, like a table or a corner of their bedroom, to prayer. Keep a Bible there, along with a cross or holy image, a candle, and incense. Make it appealing and beautiful so that you want to spend time in your prayer space.

When? Prayer becomes a good habit when we set aside time for it. Think about when you could carve out some time in your day for prayer—perhaps in the morning on the way to school, during your lunch break, or before going to sleep.

How? There are countless ways to pray. You can pray through Sacred Scripture, the Rosary, or meditation; through prayer that is vocal or silent; through prayer that praises God or asks for what you need. Don't worry too much about the how—just do it. God has already met you more than halfway.

63 Article The Lord's Prayer

In Luke's Gospel, the disciples ask Jesus to teach them to pray (see 11:1). Jesus responds with what has become the best-known and best-loved of all Christian prayers—the Lord's Prayer, also known as the Our Father. In it Jesus neatly summarizes the key elements of the Gospel message (see *CCC*, 2774): praise of God the Father's holy name, desire for the Kingdom, prayer that our needs will be met, and a plea for forgiveness.

The Lord's Prayer Teaches Us about God

Christian prayer is always Trinitarian. This means that most often Christian prayer is addressed *to* the Father, the First Person of the Trinity; *in the name of* Jesus, the Second Person of the Trinity; and *through the power of* the Holy Spirit, the Third Person of the Trinity. Because the Lord's Prayer is clearly addressed to the First Person of the Blessed Trinity, it speaks of our belief in a Triune God.

The Lord's Prayer also teaches us that Jesus, the Eternal Son of God, who assumed human nature, has revealed God the Father to us. In his earthly life, Jesus called his Divine Father *Abba*. *Abba* is a respectful term that means "Father." In teaching us to pray in the words of the Lord's Prayer, he invites us to share in that relationship of intimacy and love as adopted sons and daughters through Baptism. Indeed, praying the Lord's Prayer brings us into closer communion with the Blessed Trinity, enabling us to experience the wonder and joy of that divine life of Father, Son, and Holy Spirit.

The Lord's Prayer Teaches Us about Ourselves

Have you ever noticed how the Lord's Prayer is such an important prayer in the life of the Church? We pray it at every liturgical and sacramental celebration, including the Liturgy of the Hours, Baptism, Confirmation, and the Eucharist. This is not only because this prayer contains the words that Jesus himself taught us but also because it reflects our fundamental identity as Christians. Through Baptism we are incorporated into Christ's own Body, the Church, and adopted as children of God the Father. Praying the Lord's Prayer reminds us that as God's own adopted children, we must speak and act in a way that is worthy of this dignity. In addition, praying to our Father should develop in us the will to be like him and fosters in us a "humble and trusting heart" (*CCC*, 2800), the heart of a child who relies totally on a parent for all of her or his needs, completely trusting in that loving care. ✝

"Our Daily Bread": Catholic Relief Services

"Give us this day our daily bread." Do you sometimes just glide by that phrase of the Lord's Prayer without really considering its meaning? When we pray these words, we cannot simply ask God that our own needs be met. Rather, we must think of our sisters and brothers who suffer from a lack of "daily bread." "The drama of hunger in the world calls Christians who pray sincerely to exercise responsibility . . . both in their personal behavior and in their solidarity with the human family" (*CCC*, 2831).

One organization that works to ensure that all people have access to "daily bread" is Catholic Relief Services (CRS), the official international humanitarian agency of the United States Catholic community. CRS sponsors efforts in more than a hundred countries around the world where people suffer from lack of adequate food, nutrition, shelter, and health care. CRS always responds quickly to natural disasters like earthquakes, floods, and famines. CRS also initiates long-term projects to help local people become more self-sustaining. For example, CRS teaches people to grow their own vegetables, to practice proper sanitation, to start small businesses, and to send their children to school. In these and countless other ways, CRS lives out the words of the Lord's Prayer, creating conditions for daily bread that will endure for generations to come.

The next time you pray the Lord's Prayer, pause after "our daily bread." Remember all those whose basic needs are not met. Ask God to show you how you can help to ease poverty and hunger, both in your own community and around the world.

64 Jesus Teaches Us about Prayer

Article

In the Gospels, Jesus teaches us about prayer through the example of his actions and through his words.

Taking Time for Prayer

In his earthly life, Jesus often took time alone to pray. For example, early in Mark's Gospel, the Evangelist recounts the actions of Jesus after a very busy day of teaching and healing in the town of Capernaum: "Rising very early before dawn, he left and went off to a deserted place, where he prayed" (1:35). Later in the Book of Mark, Jesus asks the Apostles to come away with him "to a deserted place and rest a while" (6:31). However, crowds of people follow them, and Jesus, moved with compassion, teaches them and feeds them. When the people at last disperse, Jesus goes off by himself "to the mountain to pray" (6:46). Luke's Gospel also tells us that despite the great crowds that assembled to listen to Jesus and be healed by him, Jesus would make the effort to "withdraw to deserted places to pray" (5:16).

These Gospel accounts make clear that Jesus needed prayer to sustain him in his ministry. He consciously made time for it, often by getting up very early and finding a place where he could be alone. Our days too can be busy. It can be challenging for us to find a time and a place to pray. But the example of Jesus teaches us that prayer is not a luxury—it

Pray It!

Teach Us to Pray!

Lord, teach us to pray. Give us the heart and the humility to speak in our own words with you about our hopes and fears, joys and sorrows, weaknesses and strengths. Help us to be honest with ourselves and sincere before you. Teach us to listen. Guide us to see more clearly the gifts you have given us and the good ways we can use them.

Lord, fill us with great desires to speak with you. Stir within us a holy ambition to spread your word to others and to work to share your message with the world. Give us the strength to be constant in our prayer so that we may rely on you as our great friend throughout our lives. Amen.

is a necessity. The *Catechism* states that "prayer and *Christian life* are *inseparable*" (2745). This means that prayer is the strong foundation on which all the other aspects of our lives can rest—studies, work, activities, and relationships. Without prayer our daily lives can become overburdened or meaningless. With prayer our every thought, word, and deed can be transformed, directed toward loving service of God and neighbor.

The Parable of the Pharisee and the Tax Collector (Luke 18:9–18)

If you are not familiar with this brief parable, take a moment to read it now. Like many of the parables, this one contains a surprise. The Pharisees were a group within the Jewish community of Jesus' time who were very concerned with strictly following the Law of Moses. Tax collectors were hated agents of the Roman occupying forces. Jesus' listeners would have assumed that the person who "went home justified" (Luke 18:14) would be the Pharisee. But Jesus overturns their expectations. It is the tax collector who offers the authentic, humble prayer of a person seeking God's gracious mercy: "O God, be merciful to me, a sinner" (18:13).

Notice the specific audience to whom Jesus addressed this parable: "to those who were convinced of their own righteousness and despised everyone else" (18:9). Could this be us? Are we sometimes overly convinced of our own goodness? Are we completely certain that our thoughts and actions are pleasing to God? If so, we have fallen into the same trap as the Pharisee in the parable, who thanks God that he is "not like the rest of humanity" (18:11). The reality is that all human beings sin. We all need the infinite mercy of God to flood our hearts and heal our souls. The tax collector, who approaches his prayer with humility, knows this. Do we? ✝

Jesus not only taught the importance of praying but also modeled faithful prayer. How can you make prayer a more important part of your life?

Article 65 The Cornerstones of Prayer

Participation in the sacramental life of the Church is an essential aspect of the prayer life of a Catholic. In particular, the Sacrament of the Eucharist and the Sacrament of Penance and Reconciliation, which we celebrate repeatedly throughout our lives, can be continual sources of grace to us. Through them we experience the ministry of Christ through the power of the Holy Spirit and are drawn closer to God the Father. These Sacraments should be the cornerstone of our life of prayer.

The Eucharist

Saint Thomas Aquinas called the Eucharist the "Sacrament of sacraments"[1] (*CCC*, 1211). The Second Vatican Council's *Constitution on the Sacred Liturgy* (*Sacrosanctum Concilium*, 1963) picks up on this idea by describing the Eucharist as "the summit toward which the activity of the Church is directed; it is also the source from which all of its power flows" (10). Why is celebration of the Eucharist so crucial for Catholics?

- The Eucharist unites us more fully with Christ. Just as physical food nourishes and strengthens our bodies, the food of the Eucharist sustains our spiritual lives of Christian discipleship. It "preserves, increases, and renews the life of grace received at Baptism" (*CCC*, 1392).

- The Eucharist unites us with our fellow Christians. Through Holy Communion, we deepen and renew our baptismal unity with one another as brothers and sisters in Christ Jesus. Saint Paul saw this reality when he wrote, in one of the earliest texts on the Eucharist in the New Testament: "The bread that we break, is it not a participation in the body of Christ? Because the loaf of bread is one, we, though many, are one body, for we all partake of the one loaf" (1 Corinthians 10:16–17).

- The Eucharist commits us to the poor. "To receive in truth the Body and Blood of Christ given up for us, we must recognize Christ in the poorest" (*CCC*, 1397). As we are nourished at the table of the Eucharistic feast with the Body and Blood of Christ, we must commit ourselves to nourishing those members of Christ's own Body who suffer from poverty and deprivation. The Christ whom we receive in the Eucharist is the same Christ who is present in the "least ones" (Matthew 25:45): the hungry, the thirsty, the sick, the naked, the stranger, and the prisoner.

Penance and Reconciliation

The Sacrament of Penance and Recon-ciliation must also be a regular part of the prayer life of a Catholic. Though the Church asks, minimally, that we confess serious sin once a year, celebrating this Sacrament more often gives us the chance to experience the consolation and healing of God's grace and mercy. When we confess our sin to a priest, we admit that we have harmed other people and damaged our bond with the Body of Christ, the Church. The words of absolution forgive us, heal us, and welcome us back to our rightful place "in the communion of saints"[2] (*CCC*, 1469). ✝

© Bill Wittman/www.wpwittman.com

In the Sacrament of Penance and Reconciliation, the priest continues the ministry of forgiveness entrusted by Christ to the Apostles.

Live It!

When Is the Sacrament of Penance and Reconciliation Available?

Do you know how and when your parish provides opportunities to celebrate the Sacrament of Penance and Reconciliation? Parishes have set times for celebrating this Sacrament. It might be Saturday mornings or afternoons, or Wednesday evenings, for example. You may contact your pastor or another priest to request a time to celebrate the Sacrament. Another option is to participate in a communal celebration that includes an opportunity for individual confession and absolution. Many parishes have these celebrations during Lent and Advent. Check your parish's bulletin for information about the celebration of the Sacrament of Penance and Reconciliation in your parish.

Celebrating the Sacrament of Penance and Reconciliation

Has it been awhile since you celebrated the Sacrament of Penance and Reconciliation? Are you afraid you have forgotten how? If so, here is a quick review:

- **Greeting and Welcome:** The priest with whom you are celebrating the Sacrament welcomes you, makes the Sign of the Cross with you, and reminds you of God's infinite mercy.
- **Confession of Sin:** You tell the priest your sins. He may offer you spiritual advice or guidance.
- **Penance:** The priest gives you a penance, which will help to repair the harm your sin has caused and help you to grow in your life of Christian discipleship. A penance could be a prayer, a good work, or some other type of offering.
- **Act of Contrition:** You express sorrow for your sins. There are many versions of this prayer, or you can make up your own, praying with the words of your own heart.
- **Absolution:** The priest speaks the words of absolution. He offers you God's pardon and peace through the ministry of the Church.
- **Conclusion:** The priest asks you to "go in peace."

^{Article}
66 Do Catholics Pray to Mary?

The belief that Catholics worship Mary and the saints is a common misunderstanding. In fact, Catholics worship only the Blessed Trinity, for only our Triune God is worthy of adoration. Besides, we know that only God can answer our prayers, so we never ask Mary or any other saint to answer our prayers as we would ask God to do. We do, however, ask Mary to intercede for us, and we honor her as the Mother of God.

Mary, Our Intercessor

When Catholics offer prayers directed to Mary, such as the Hail Mary, we are asking for Mary's intercessory help. Just as we ask our faith-filled friends on earth to pray for us, we can also ask our friends in Heaven to pray for us, and Mary is surely one of those friends.

Our prayer to Mary is really a prayer that she will offer that same prayer to God on our behalf. Because she is already in Heaven, she knows better than us how best to offer prayer to God.

In her earthly life, Mary cooperated completely with God's plan for our salvation. She became a model of true discipleship for us. Our prayers to Mary acknowledge that in her heavenly life, she can continue to do good with us and for us.

Honoring Mary

Although Catholics worship God alone, we venerate Mary and the saints. Venerating means showing honor, respect, and devotion. Catholics venerate Mary with various titles, the foremost of which is Mother of God. We celebrate various feasts and solemnities in her honor, like her Immaculate Conception, on December 8; the Annunciation, on March 25; and her Assumption, on August 15. We also have many traditions of prayer and devotion associated with Mary, such as **litanies, novenas,** the wearing of medals, and the Rosary. Our veneration of Mary through these and other practices honors the unique role she played in God's plan of salvation and brings us closer to her Son. ✝

litanies
Prayers consisting of a series of invocations and responses.

novenas
From the Latin word for "nine," they are public or private devotions that extend for a period of nine days.

The *Magnificat*

One way we can truly pray *with* Mary is to pray in her own words. Saint Luke's Gospel gives us her prayer, the *Magnificat*, also called the Canticle of Mary (see 1:46–55).

When Mary finds out she will be the mother of Jesus, the first thing she does is visit her cousin Elizabeth. The two women—one old, one young, and both pregnant through a miracle of God's grace—rejoice together. In this context Mary offers her *Magnificat*. In it, she praises the "Mighty One" (Luke 1:49) who has done great things for her and whose gracious mercy has turned the world upside down. The God she "magnifies" is the One who fills the hungry but sends the rich away and who lifts up the lowly but throws down the powerful.

© Brooklyn Museum/Corbis

At the time when Mary prayed the *Magnificat*, her people, suffering under Roman oppression, were longing for justice. When we pray in her words, we not only honor Mary, we also stand in solidarity with all those suffering people today who live in the hope that God will, one day, do "great things" (Luke 1:49) for them.

Part Review

1. What is prayer?

2. What is a prayer of petition? What is an intercessory prayer?

3. What does the Lord's Prayer teach us about God?

4. What does the Lord's Prayer teach us about ourselves?

5. What do Jesus' actions teach us about prayer?

6. Why are the Eucharist and the Sacrament of Penance and Reconciliation so crucial for Catholics?

7. If only God can answer prayers, why do we pray to Mary and other saints?

Part 3

We Respond through a Life of Discipleship

The word *disciple* comes from the Latin word for "student" or "pupil." The disciples whom Jesus called to accompany him in his earthly life learned from all his words and actions. Jesus' whole life was a model for living a holy life. In fact, some Gospel texts refer to Jesus as *rabbi,* which is Hebrew for "teacher."

Being a disciple of Jesus today means dedicating our whole lives to him and basing our decisions on his words and actions too. We follow his example of total self-giving by serving others. We seek forgiveness when we sin, and we extend forgiveness to those who harm us, just as Jesus forgave his killers from the cross. We share the Good News of the Gospel with all those we meet, trusting that God is ever at work in our efforts to witness to our faith.

The topics covered is this part are:

- Article 67: "Mary: First Disciple and Model of Faith" (page 213)

- Article 68: "Discipleship: Resisting Evil, Seeking Forgiveness" (page 215)

- Article 69: "Discipleship: Concern for the Common Good" (page 217)

- Article 70: "Discipleship: The Call to Evangelization" (page 220)

Article 67 Mary: First Disciple and Model of Faith

As we seek to respond to Jesus with a life of authentic Christian discipleship, the lives of the many holy women and men who have gone before us can be models for us. Foremost among these models is Mary, the Mother of Jesus.

The First Disciple

As Jesus' own mother, Mary was among the first people to believe in him and to follow him as a disciple. We see evidence of this in New Testament texts. For example, in the story of the wedding at Cana (see John 2:1–11), Mary instructs the servers to "do whatever he tells you" (verse 5). She clearly believes Jesus can and will reveal his glory through a miracle, or "sign." In fact, he does, by turning water into wine: "Jesus did this as the beginning of his signs in Cana in Galilee and so revealed his glory, and his disciples began to believe in him" (verse 11).

After Jesus' death, Resurrection, and Ascension, Mary gathers with the community of believers in Jerusalem who eventually became the Church: "All these devoted themselves with one accord to prayer, together with some women, and Mary the mother of Jesus, and his brothers" (Acts of the Apostles 1:14). Because this is before Pentecost, Mary is "imploring the gift of the Spirit" (*Dogmatic Constitution on the Church* [*Lumen Gentium*, 1964], 59) to be poured out upon them. In fact, we can safely say that Mary "aided the beginnings of the church by her prayers" (69). For this reason she is herself not only the first disciple but also the Mother of all other disciples. She is the Mother of the Church.

Model of Faith

The *Catechism* states that "by her complete adherence to the Father's will, to his Son's redemptive work, and to every prompting of the Holy Spirit, the Virgin Mary is the Church's model of faith and charity" (967). We must remember that Mary was not a passive pawn in the hands of God. She was not a puppet whose every word and action God controlled;

Annunciation

The visit of the Angel Gabriel to the Virgin Mary to announce to her that she is to be the Mother of the Savior.

rather, Mary's faith led her to an active, free choice to cooperate with God's plan for our salvation.

When the angel Gabriel appears to Mary in the **Annunciation,** she questions him, seeking to understand how it could be possible for a virgin to have a child. She ultimately says yes, even though it is likely she does not fully understand all she is taking on. As the years go by, she watches her Son grow up and fulfill his mission of salvation. When that mission reaches its completion, she courageously stays by Jesus' side as he suffers the shameful, violent, and torturous death of a condemned criminal. At every turn, her trust in God's goodness and her surrender to his will make her a model of faith for us.

Mary's role in salvation history places her in a long line of courageous and holy women who, in their own way and their own time, cooperated with God's plan for their people. These women include Deborah, the judge; Ruth, the Moabite daughter-in-law of Naomi; Hannah, the mother of Samuel; Judith, the widow and warrior; and Esther, the Persian queen (see *CCC,* 489). These women are Mary's foremothers in faith. Like her, they confidently hoped for God's deliverance. Among this company of women, Mary stands out as unique, for "after a long period of waiting for the promise, the times are fulfilled" (*Church,* 55). In Mary the divine plan reaches its definitive moment as the Eternal Son of God takes on human flesh in her very body. Because of this she is also truly the Mother of God. ✝

This mosaic is from a chapel in the Church of the Assumption in Jerusalem. Which of these six women from the Old Testament can you identify from their images?

© Bill Wittman/www.wpwittman.com

Article 68 Discipleship: Resisting Evil, Seeking Forgiveness

In our lives of Christian discipleship, we must open ourselves to God's grace so we can resist sin and evil as best we can. When we give in to the temptations of sin, that same divine grace helps us to seek forgiveness for our failings.

Resisting Evil

God has given us the gift of freedom, or free will. This means God never forces us to choose the good. We must freely decide for ourselves. However, the grace of Jesus' death and Resurrection has made us adopted children of God the Father and has given us a new life in the Holy Spirit. This new life delivers us from the power of sin, making it easier for us to choose the good and resist evil. When we believe in Jesus and in the saving power of his death and Resurrection, we are strengthened to follow the example of his words and deeds. In "acting rightly and doing good" (CCC, 1709), we become holy: "The disciple attains the perfection of charity which is holiness. Having matured in grace, the moral life blossoms into eternal life in the glory of heaven" (1709).

Seeking Forgiveness

None of us will ever resist sin and evil every single time we are confronted with it. We are imperfect creatures. Sinful behaviors can seem attractive to us when our minds and hearts are misguided, divided, or disordered. When we give in to temptation, Jesus teaches us to repent, to turn ourselves back toward him, seeking forgiveness and a new start.

In order to experience the mercy and forgiveness of God, we must freely admit our sin. The First Letter of John puts it this way: "If we say, 'We are without sin,' we deceive ourselves, and the truth is not in us. If we acknowledge our sins, he is faithful and just and will forgive our sins and cleanse us from every wrongdoing" (1:8–9). The *Catechism* uses the image of a doctor treating a patient to describe the way grace can heal our sin, once we have confessed it: "To do its work grace must uncover sin so as to convert our hearts. . . . Like a physician who probes the wound before treating

Pope John Paul II

Forgiveness was one of the hallmarks of the papacy of John Paul II, who served as Pope from 1978 until his death in 2005.

As the head of the Church, John Paul II sought forgiveness from groups of people whom members of the Church had harmed. His 1998 statement "We Remember: A Reflection on the Shoah" expresses sorrow for the failure of Christians to save more Jews during the Holocaust. It states: "The spiritual resistance and concrete action of other Christians was not that which might have been expected from Christ's followers. . . . For Christians, this heavy burden of conscience of their brothers and sisters during the Second World War must be a call to penitence." As part of the celebration of the Jubilee Year 2000, John Paul II offered a sweeping apology for errors and misdeeds done by members of the Church throughout history in a document titled "Memory and Reconciliation: The Church and the Faults of the Past." In 2002 he apologized to those who had been victims of sexual abuse by priests.

These pleas for forgiveness, on behalf of the Church, were matched by John Paul II's extraordinary ability to extend forgiveness when he had been harmed. On May 13, 1981, John Paul II was shot by Mehmet Ali Agca while greeting crowds of people at the Vatican. After six hours of surgery, John Paul II made a request: "Pray for the brother who shot me, whom I have sincerely forgiven." Two years later he visited Ali Agca in prison, assuring him of his forgiveness and arranging for his eventual legal pardon.

it, God, by his Word and by his Spirit, casts a living light on sin" (1848).

When we have admitted our sin—brought it out of the darkness and into the marvelous light of God's mercy—God can truly heal us, forgive us, and put us back on the path of Christian discipleship. Though we can confess our sins to God and ask for forgiveness at any time, doing so within the context of the Sacrament of Penance and Reconciliation reminds us that we are part of a community of faith, a community harmed by the sin of any one of its members. This Sacrament seals us with the gift of God's pardon and peace and strengthens us in our life of faith. ✝

Article 69 Discipleship: Concern for the Common Good

Although our life of Christian discipleship must be rooted in prayer and in a close relationship with Jesus Christ, it cannot end there. When we are truly in communion with Jesus, we are attuned to his presence in the "least ones" (Matthew 25:45) and moved to serve them in his name. Indeed, active involvement in the world is a key element of our baptismal call.

The Church teachings that guide our efforts to create a more just and peaceful world are called Catholic Social Teaching (CST). The *Catechism* describes CST as "a body of

Pray It!

Act of Contrition

My God, I am sorry for my sins with all my heart.
In choosing to do wrong and failing to do good,
I have sinned against you
whom I should love above all things.
I firmly intend, with your help,
to do penance, to sin no more,
and to avoid whatever leads me to sin.
Our Savior Jesus Christ suffered and died for us.
In his name, my God, have mercy.
Amen.

(Rite of Penance)

doctrine, which is articulated as the Church interprets events in the course of history, with the assistance of the Holy Spirit, in the light of the whole of what has been revealed by Jesus Christ"[3] (2422). Though the tenets of CST are rooted in the Gospel message, Catholics credit Pope Leo XIII as the first Church leader to address the issue directly. His encyclical *On the Condition of Labor (Rerum Novarum)* was issued in 1891. Since that time several key principles have emerged as crucial elements of CST. Various lists of the principles may differ in the way topics are grouped, but all include the following key points.

- **Human dignity.** All human life is sacred and must be respected and protected at all times.

- **Community and the common good.** We must be concerned about not only our own success and well-being but also the common good of all people, especially those most in need.

- **Rights and responsibilities.** We all have the right to life and to life's basic needs, like food, shelter, and health care. We also have the duty to ensure these rights are always protected.

- **Option for the poor and vulnerable.** The needs of the poor must have first priority in how we spend our time, money, and other resources.

- **Participation.** All persons have a right to participate in the cultural, economic, and political life of society.

- **Dignity of work and rights of workers.** Workers have a right to a fair wage and to decent working conditions. They have the right to organize and join unions and to go on strike when these basic rights are not being respected.

Catholic Wisdom

Learn More about Catholic Social Teaching (CST)

To learn more about the main themes of CST, look for the United States bishops' document "Sharing Catholic Social Teaching: Challenges and Directions." You can find it on the Web site of the United States Conference of Catholic Bishops and possibly in your school library.

Saint John Baptist de La Salle

Saint John Baptist de La Salle was born into a wealthy family in Reims, France, in 1651. As a young man, he studied theology and was ordained a priest in 1678.

In seventeenth-century France, there were many poor people, but only the rich could afford to provide schooling for their children. De La Salle was moved by the plight of the poor he saw every day. He became determined to provide them with access to education. He believed that despite the poverty of their circumstances, they had a basic human right to better their lives. Eventually his passion for education became his only priority, and he renounced his family wealth to devote himself fully to it. He lived in community with the companions he had recruited to teach with him. Together they offered education to all children, regardless of families' ability to pay. These companions eventually became the members of a new religious order, the Brothers of the Christian Schools, also known as the Christian Brothers. Before De La Salle died in 1719, they had created a network of schools all across France.

Today more than 900,000 students are taught in Lasallian schools, sponsored by the Christian Brothers in more than eighty countries around the globe. The mission of each of these schools is in keeping with De La Salle's original vision: to give a human and Christian education to the young, especially the poor.

De La Salle's feast day is April 7.

- **Stewardship of creation.** We must protect the resources of our planet, preserving them for future generations.
- **Solidarity.** We must support and care for one another as brothers and sisters in one human family, dwelling around the globe.
- **Role of government.** Governments must protect human life and human rights, promote human dignity, and build the common good.
- **Promotion of peace.** As Pope John Paul II put it, "Peace is not just the absence of war." We must promote peace as the positive presence of respect, collaboration, and justice.

Which of these principles of Catholic Social Teaching do you think most needs to be promoted in our world? in our country? in your school? ✝

In working for the common good, we participate in Christ's ministry of love and healing. As a disciple of Christ, how do you work for the common good?

Article 70 Discipleship: The Call to Evangelization

When you see a good movie or hear a great song, you want to share it with others. It is natural to want to share something exciting and wonderful. That is exactly what we are called to do when we hear the message of the Gospel.

© Con Tanasiuk/Design Pics/Corbis

As baptized Christians we have been given the mission of sharing the Good News of Jesus Christ with all those we meet. This "proclamation of Christ by word and the testimony of life"[4] (*CCC*, 905) is called **evangelization.** *Evangelization* comes from the Greek word *euangelion*, which means "good news." Because the life, death, and Resurrection of Jesus is truly Good News for all humanity, we want to share it with others.

evangelization
The proclamation of the Gospel of Jesus Christ through word and witness.

Jesus Missions the Disciples

We can see the roots of our call to evangelize in the mission Jesus gives to the disciples. For example, in the Gospel of Luke (see 10:1–20), Jesus sends out seventy-two disciples in pairs. He directs them to the cities and towns he intends to visit, asking them to teach and heal in his name. They return from their mission rejoicing at all they have been able to accomplish. In the same way, in the Gospel of Matthew, the Risen Christ commissions the eleven Apostles with these famous words: "Go, therefore, and make disciples of all nations, baptizing them in the name of the Father, and of the Son, and of the holy Spirit, teaching them to observe all that I have commanded you" (28:19–20). These Apostles try to carry out this mission, and, when their death draws near, they appoint successors. In this way the work of evangelization can continue "until the end of the age" (28:20).

Jesus Missions Us

Jesus has entrusted us with the same mission of evangelization as the original disciples. It is possible, "in the ordinary circumstances of the world"[5] (*CCC*, 905), to bear authentic witness to our faith in Jesus. This witness may, in time, lead others to faith in him. For example, we can pray regularly; share generously, especially with the poor; and speak freely and without embarrassment of our Christian faith. In these efforts God will surely give us courage and wisdom so that, in our words and actions, "the power of the Gospel may shine out" (*Church*, 35).

Evangelizing, Not Proselytizing

missionaries
Those people who devote themselves to spreading the Gospel—in word and service—to those who have not heard it or to those who have rejected it; missionaries often serve in foreign countries.

In some Christian denominations, the mission to evangelize has become distorted by proselytism, the active, even aggressive, seeking of converts to one's own religion, often away from another religion. With the best of intentions (the salvation of souls), those who proselytize will sometimes relentlessly pursue people, even those who have never shown interest in their message.

Today the Catholic approach to evangelization is different. We recognize that God calls each person to an authentic relationship with him. We know that we must be "on the lookout for occasions to proclaim Christ by word, either to unbelievers . . . or to the faithful" (*Decree on the Apostolate of Lay People [Apostolicam Actuositatem]*, 6). However, we also recognize that we must respect people's basic freedom to accept or reject the Gospel message. The witness of our faithful lives and our proclamation of the Good News may not have any immediate effect on another person. However, we trust that God is at work all the same, in ways we cannot fully understand, and that slowly, even without being noticed, the Gospel is spreading throughout the world. ✝

Live It!

Go and Make Disciples

In 1990 the United States Conference of Catholic Bishops unveiled a plan for a renewed effort of evangelization titled *Go and Make Disciples*. It presented three goals:

Goal 1: To bring about in all Catholics such an enthusiasm for their faith that, in living their faith in Jesus, they freely share it with others.

Goal 2: To invite all people in the United States, whatever their social or cultural background, to hear the message of salvation in Jesus Christ so they may come to join us in the fullness of the Catholic faith.

Goal 3: To foster Gospel values in our society, promoting the dignity of the human person, the importance of the family, and the common good of our society, so that our nation may continue to be transformed by the saving power of Jesus Christ.

(Go and Make Disciples, 46, 53, and 56)

Reflect on these goals and consider how you can live them out in your life and how you might help others to learn about the Church's social teaching.

Maryknoll: Evangelizing in Mission

Maryknoll is a Catholic organization, based in the United States, that sends sisters, brothers, priests, and lay **missionaries** overseas to engage in works of service, justice, and evangelization. Since its founding in 1911, members of Maryknoll have witnessed to the Gospel of Jesus Christ by working with refugees in war zones; ministering to the sick, elderly, and orphans; and building communities of faith. Most missionaries serve in a particular location in Africa, Asia, or Latin America for three or four years. Others decide to give their whole lives to this ministry.

Maryknoll missionaries use their words and their deeds "to announce and to give witness to the Good News of the Reign of God." However, their proclamation of the Gospel message takes account of the needs of the whole person—both body and soul. It also deeply respects human freedom, which, as part of our inherent dignity, is God's gracious gift. Regardless of whether a particular person chooses to embrace the Good News of Jesus Christ, the missionary trusts that he or she has planted seeds of faith that, one day, may bear fruit.

Part Review

1. Why is Mary called the first disciple of Jesus?

2. How is Mary a model of faith for us?

3. How does the grace of Jesus' death and Resurrection empower us to resist sin and evil?

4. Why is the Sacrament of Penance and Reconciliation important?

5. What is Catholic Social Teaching (CST)?

6. Describe three principles of CST.

7. How is the Catholic approach to evangelization different from proselytizing?

Part 4

Our Response to Jesus Matters

If you are like many people, you may have sometimes wondered if believing in Jesus makes any real difference. In the end does it really matter what we believe or in whom we believe?

The answer is a definitive yes—it matters a lot! Our response to Jesus during our lives on earth shapes the ultimate destiny of our lives in Heaven. If we seek to follow him though faithful lives of prayer and discipleship in the company of the Church, we will share in all that Jesus has promised us: new and resurrected life, union with the Blessed Trinity, and a vision of our Triune God in heavenly glory.

Jesus wants us to experience all these good things. However, at all times we remain utterly free people. We are free to accept or reject the grace and blessings he offers to us. If we exercise our freedom wisely, we can make choices that bring us closer to the ultimate destiny Jesus desires for all of us: eternal life and happiness with him in Heaven.

The topics covered is this part are:

Article 71 Our Destiny: Union with God

We are created and destined to be fully united with God forever. God wants this so much that he sent his Son to redeem us so we can share a life of love with him eternally. Even in our earthly lives, we experience a degree of union with God through our participation in the Sacraments and through our efforts to follow a path of holiness. If our earthly lives are faithful, we will attain our final destiny: complete union with the Blessed Trinity.

Faith: The Way to Our Destiny

"Believing in Jesus Christ and in the One who sent him for our salvation is necessary for obtaining that salvation"[6] (*CCC*, 161). In other words, without faith, we cannot have salvation. Faith in Jesus is our path to eternal life. It assures us that we will one day enjoy the company of the Blessed Trinity and all the angels and saints. Faith is an act of the entire Church. The faith of the Church is an important part of the faith of every member of the Body of Christ, and it calls forth our faith and nurtures and supports our belief in God. Saint Thomas Aquinas described faith as "a foretaste of the knowledge that will make us blessed in the life to come" (Saint Thomas Aquinas, *Comp. theol.* 1, 2) (*CCC*, 184). The blessedness of the afterlife to which Saint Thomas referred is called the Beatific Vision.

The Beatific Vision

The Beatific Vision is the vision of God in Heaven after we die—the "contemplation of God in his heavenly glory" (*CCC*, 1028). Whether we acknowledge it or not, the desire to see God, to know God, is built into us. Because of this, the Beatific Vision is the ultimate goal of our lives. When the journey of our earthly lives is complete, God opens the divine mystery to us. He gives us the capacity to contemplate, understand, and appreciate his heavenly glory.

Although no one has come back to earth from Heaven to tell us what the Beatific Vision is like, several New Testament passages refer to it. In the Beatitudes, Jesus proclaims: "Blessed are the clean of heart, / for they will see God"

Preaching the Gospel in Word and Deed

If faith in the Gospel message is necessary for salvation through Jesus Christ, then the Church must be willing to preach that message in all places and circumstances. Church history provides us with many examples of people who have been willing to share the Gospel message through faithful witness to the truth and through courageous acts of service:

- Saint Francis Xavier, a Jesuit priest, brought the Gospel to India and Japan in the mid-sixteenth century. At that time many Asian countries were closed to the West. He was en route to China when he became seriously ill and died.

- Fr. Matteo Ricci, also a Jesuit, had spent nearly three decades in China by the time of his death in 1610. He worked to gain acceptance among the local people. He encouraged them to see links between Christianity and Chinese cultural traditions.

- Blessed Damien de Veuster (pictured below), a Belgian priest, ministered among the lepers on the Hawaiian island of Molokai for nearly twenty years. He willingly lived and worked with the people without fear or prejudice. This led to his own death from leprosy in 1889. His associate, Blessed Marianne Cope, continued this ministry after his death.

- Fr. Stanley Rother, a native of Oklahoma City, served the Mayan people in the village of Santiago Atitlan, Guatemala, for thirteen years during that country's bloody civil war. Father Stanley stood with the people of his parish against a repressive government. For this he was murdered in 1981.

- Four women—Maryknoll Sisters Maura Clarke and Ita Ford, Ursuline Sister Dorothy Kazel, and lay missioner Jean Donovan—were killed in El Salvador in 1980 because of their fidelity to the Gospel message, especially the Church's preferential option for the poor.

Few of us will actually travel to distant lands for the sake of the Gospel. But we can be inspired by those who have. Their example can help us as we seek to share the saving message of Christ in our ordinary, day-to-day lives.

© CORBIS

(Matthew 5:8). Similarly, Saint Paul writes in his First Letter to the Corinthians: "At present we see indistinctly, as in a mirror, but then face to face. At present I know partially; then I shall know fully, as I am fully known" (13:12). Finally, the First Letter of John says that "we shall be like him, for we shall see him as he is" (3:2).

Some of the early Church Fathers also wrote about the Beatific Vision. For example, Saint Augustine described it in this way: "God himself will be the goal of our desires; we shall contemplate him without end, love him without surfeit, praise him without weariness. This gift, this state, this act, like eternal life itself, will assuredly be common to all"[7] (CCC, 2550). As we live our earthly lives, these reflections on the Beatific Vision help us to keep the ultimate goal of our heavenly life in mind. ✝

laity
All members of the Church with the exception of those who are ordained as bishops, priests, or deacons. The laity share in Christ's role as priest, prophet, and king, witnessing to God's love and power in the world.

Article 72 The Church: Visible and Spiritual

Our baptismal call to live lives of faithful discipleship does not happen in isolation. We are members of the Church, the Body of Christ, brothers and sisters to one another. There is a visible reality of the Church that is clear to all, but there is also an invisible, spiritual reality that is known only through the eyes of faith. This invisible reality is often described as the Mystical Body of Christ and as the Communion of Saints.

The Mystical Body of Christ

When we are baptized into Christ and become members of his Body, the Church, we become part of both a visible, human society and an invisible, divine reality. The visible aspect of the Church is easy for us to see. For example, we can study history to see the Church's presence and involvement in human affairs. We can look to the present day and the many ministries of the Church in parishes, schools, hospitals, and social service agencies. We can also simply look around us to see one another. The visible organization of the Church includes hierarchical leaders, ordained ministers, members of religious orders, and the **laity.**

The invisible reality of the Church is more difficult to perceive: in fact, it can be seen from a perspective of faith only.

This spiritual component of the Church is called the Mystical Body of Christ. The *Catechism* describes the Mystical Body of Christ as a "supernatural unity . . . a single mystical person"[8] (1474). This means that all members of the Church are truly and spiritually united as one Body in the divine life of the Blessed Trinity. The members include those living on earth, those being purified in Purgatory, and those living in Heaven. Think about that: Nothing can separate us from the Mystical Body of which we are a part, not even death.

The Communion of Saints

Although we often think of saints as only those people who have been officially canonized, or recognized, as such by the Church, a saint is really anyone who is trying to live a holy and Christian life, through the grace of Christ. This includes those of us who are living on earth, those who have died and are being purified in Purgatory, and those who are, even now, dwelling in the glory of God's holy presence in Heaven. This union of all God's holy ones—on earth, in Purgatory, and in Heaven—is called the Communion of Saints.

As the Communion of Saints, we are united "in holy things" and "among holy persons" (*CCC*, 948). The "holy things" in which we are united are the Sacraments, especially the Eucharist, and other spiritual gifts. The "holy persons" with whom we are joined as one are all those members of Christ's own Body, the great "cloud of witnesses" (Hebrews

Pray It!

Prayer Partners

Many people have a friend who is a prayer partner. This is someone they pray with and for. Each one of us is blessed, in a way, with a countless number of prayer partners in the Communion of Saints. Especially when we are gathered for the Sacrament of the Eucharist, we pray with, to, and for the Communion of Saints. One of the optional prayers at Mass, called the *Confiteor*, reflects the unity of all who are part of the Communion of Saints: "I ask blessed Mary, ever Virgin, all the Angels and Saints, and you, my brothers and sisters, to pray for me to the Lord our God" (Roman Missal).

The next time you participate in the Mass, take a moment to call to mind all those who are united with you. Recognize that your prayers are joined with the prayers of the entire Church, past and present. In the Communion of Saints, each one of us is blessed with amazing prayer partners.

What invisible spiritual reality is signified by the visible sign of being immersed in the waters of Baptism?

© Fabio Corral/CORBIS

12:1) who have faithfully kept their "eyes fixed on Jesus, the leader and perfecter of faith" (12:2). ✝

^{Article}73 The Christian Understanding of Death

Just as our response to Jesus affects every aspect of our daily living, it also affects our approach to death and dying.

The Resurrection of the Body

God created human beings with both bodies and souls. At the moment when the physical body dies, the soul separates from the body and goes to meet God. At the Final Judgment, when Christ comes again in glory, the soul will be reunited with the body in a new and glorified state. Our bodily resurrection has been a central truth of Christian faith from the beginning. It is consistently proclaimed in every book of the New Testament and even in some books of the Old Testament. For example, in the Second Book of Maccabees, a mother speaks to her seven sons who are facing martyrdom because of their fidelity to the Jewish law: "I do not know how you came into existence in my womb; it was not I who gave you the breath of life. . . . Therefore, since it is the

Creator of the universe who shapes each man's beginning, as he brings about the origin of everything, he, in his mercy, will give you back both breath and life" (7:22–23). This courageous woman recognizes that God, the Author of all life, will surely bring her sons to a new and eternal life that is both physical and spiritual.

"By Your Cross and Resurrection, You Have Set Us Free"

We proclaim these words in the Memorial Acclamation at a Eucharistic liturgy. We mean that Jesus' death has forever changed death into something positive. If you have been to a Catholic funeral, you may recall hearing this prayer: "Lord, for your faithful people life is changed, not ended. When the body of our earthly dwelling lies in death we gain an everlasting dwelling place in heaven"[9] (*CCC,* 1012). Because Christians enter into the death of Christ in Baptism, our physical death allows us to share in the glory of his Resurrection. That is surely a good thing!

Preparing for Death

Have you ever prayed the words of the Hail Mary—"pray for us sinners, now and at the hour of our death"? If so, then

Live It!

Start with the End in Mind

Have you ever heard the phrase "start with the end in mind"? This means that before you begin something, you decide what end result you would like. Whether you are writing an essay, planning a mission trip, or going sightseeing, you can have a better experience if you have the end result in mind. It would be a shame to be in Paris and really want to see the Eiffel Tower but never see it because you got sidetracked.

What does this have to do with death? The truth is we have a limited time on earth. Eventually our earthly life will end. We are called, though, to a greater end—eternal life with God in Heaven. How would your life be different if you made your decisions with the goal of Heaven in mind? Start each day by asking yourself the following questions:

- What can I do today to grow closer to God?
- What can I do today to help others recognize God's loving presence in their lives?
- What can I do today to share the Gospel message?

Cardinal Joseph Bernardin of Chicago

Cardinal Joseph Bernardin had been archbishop of Chicago for thirteen years when he was diagnosed with pancreatic cancer in June 1995. After undergoing surgery, chemotherapy, and radiation, he began a new phase of his ministry as a priest and bishop: outreach to cancer patients. He visited hundreds of people suffering with this terminal illness in hospitals, in hospices, and in their homes, and he corresponded with many more. He spoke freely with them about his own fears, his physical and emotional pain, and his sleepless nights. He encouraged them to view "death as a friend, as the transition from earthly life to life eternal" (*New York Times,* August 31, 1996). In Cardinal Bernardin these people found a true companion and ally. He was someone willing to take up the cross of cancer and journey with them through the final days of their earthly pilgrimage.

At the end of August 1996, Cardinal Bernardin announced that his cancer had returned and that he had less than a year to live. Soon it was no longer possible for him to keep up his busy schedule of public appearances and sacramental ministry, so he turned to writing. He completed his spiritual autobiography *The Gift of Peace* (Loyola Press, 1997) just days before his death on November 14, 1996.

For many people Cardinal Bernardin was a model of how to die—with grace, dignity, and faith. When asked what he expected in the afterlife, he replied: "I don't have a crystal ball, but I know the Lord's promises—to be with him and to be happy with him. In faith I know the Lord will be waiting for me and his promises will be fulfilled" (*New York Times,* August 31, 1996).

you have, in a small way, prepared for your own death. For a young person with many years ahead of you, this may sound odd, morbid, or creepy! But it is in fact something the Church encourages for people of all ages. We need to remember our mortality, the fact that we will not live on this earth forever. It helps us to "realize that we have only a limited time in which to bring our lives to fulfillment" (*CCC*, 1007). It is also a way of growing in faith, of surrendering to the divine will and trusting that our lives are truly in God's hands, from the moment of our conception to the moment of our last breath. ✝

"Pray for us now and at the hour of our death." These words remind us that our destiny lies not in this world but in eternal happiness with God in Heaven.

Article 74 Heaven, Hell, and Purgatory

After death, all people will face divine judgment twice, in the Final Judgment and in each person's Particular Judgment. The Final Judgment will occur for all of us when Jesus comes again in glory. No one but God the Father knows when that will be. At the moment of our death, we will face Christ, the judge of the living and the dead, in the Particular Judgment, which has three possible outcomes.

Heaven

Those who die in God's grace and friendship and are perfectly purified go immediately to Heaven. There they live in the company of the Blessed Trinity forever. The *Catechism* defines Heaven in various ways: as "communion of life and love with the Trinity, with the Virgin Mary, the angels, and all the blessed" (1024); as "the ultimate end and fulfillment of the deepest human longings, the state of supreme, definitive happiness" (1024); and as "the blessed community of all who are perfectly incorporated into Christ" (1026).

Though these definitions give us some glimpse into the reality of Heaven's glory, we cannot really know what Heaven is like until we are there. In fact, the idea of Heaven stretches the limits of human imagination and language. For this reason Sacred Scripture uses metaphors in an effort to give us some sense of it. These metaphors include "life, light, peace, wedding feast, wine of the kingdom, the Father's house, the heavenly Jerusalem, paradise" (*CCC*, 1027).

Hell

Because God gave us the gift of free will, he never forces us to do good. We must freely choose to do so for ourselves. "We cannot be united with God unless we freely choose to love him" (*CCC*, 1033). When we choose evil, we reject the love, grace, and redemption God offers to us, and instead choose Hell, the "state of definitive self-exclusion from communion with God and the blessed" (1033). Those in Hell are eternally separated from God. This is its "chief punishment" (1035).

God does not send anyone to Hell. Rather, through our own choices, we can send ourselves there: "By rejecting grace

Catholic Wisdom

Prayer for the Souls in Purgatory

Pope Benedict XVI wrote this about the Christian responsibility to pray for all of the souls in Purgatory:

No one lives alone. No one sins alone. No one is saved alone. The lives of others continually spill over into mine: in what I think, say, do and achieve. And conversely, my life spills over into that of others: for better and for worse. So my prayer for another is not something extraneous to that person, something external, not even after death. ("Encyclical Letter *Spe Salvi* of the Supreme Pontiff Benedict XVI to the Bishops, Priests and Deacons, Men and Women Religious, and All the Lay Faithful on Christian Hope," 48)

Dante's *Divine Comedy*

Heaven, Hell, and Purgatory have always been popular subjects for artists. Perhaps because no one living has ever experienced these realities, painters, sculptors, and writers can allow their imaginations free rein to show them creatively and vividly.

One of the most famous portrayals of Heaven, Hell, and Purgatory is in Dante's *Divine Comedy*. It is an epic poem composed by this devoutly Catholic writer in the early fourteenth century. The narrator is meant to be Dante himself. He recounts an imaginary journey he takes from the depths of Hell, through Purgatory, and finally to the paradise of Heaven. Along the way he meets people from history, literature, and his own native Florence, in Italy. He learns how these individuals' virtues and vices, strengths and weaknesses, and good and evil choices determined their final fate.

The three volumes of the *Divine Comedy*—*Inferno*, *Purgatorio*, and *Paradiso*—are considered to be classics of Western literature. They give us not only an artist's creative insight into the realities of the afterlife but also a renewed appreciation for the power of fiction and poetry to stir us to faith and to conversion.

in this life, one already judges oneself, receives according to one's works, and can even condemn oneself for all eternity by rejecting the Spirit of love"[10] (*CCC*, 679).

Purgatory

Purgatory is for those who are ultimately destined for Heaven but who are not yet pure enough to enter it. It is a state of final purification or cleansing that allows these individuals "to achieve the holiness necessary to enter the joy of heaven" (*CCC*, 1030). When we pray for the dead, we are interceding for those in Purgatory. We are asking that they may soon enjoy the everlasting glory, peace, and comfort of God's holy presence. ☦

Part Review

1. Explain why faith in Jesus is our path to eternal life.

2. Define the Beatific Vision.

3. What is the Mystical Body of Christ?

4. What is the Communion of Saints?

5. How did the death of Jesus change death for all of us?

6. Why is it good for us to keep in mind that death is inevitable?

7. What ideas and images can help us to have some understanding of Heaven?

8. What is the relationship between Hell and the gift of free will?

9. What is the purpose of Purgatory?

Glossary

A

Abba: A way of addressing God the Father used by Jesus to call attention to his—and our—intimate relationship with his Heavenly Father. *Abba* means "my Father" or "our Father" in Aramaic. *(page 174)*

Annunciation: The visit of the Angel Gabriel to the Virgin Mary to announce to her that she is to be the Mother of the Savior. *(page 214)*

anti-Semitism: Prejudice against the Jewish people. *(page 105)*

B

Beatific Vision: Direct encounter and sight of God in the glory of Heaven. *(page 98)*

beatitude: The state of eternal happiness with God in Heaven. *(page 18)*

Beatitudes: The teachings of Jesus during the Sermon on the Mount in which he describes the actions and attitudes that should characterize Christians and by which one can discover genuine meaning and happiness. *(page 173)*

C

canon of Scripture: The list of the books of the Bible officially recognized as sacred, inspired writings. *(page 63)*

canonized: A deceased Catholic's having been publicly and officially proclaimed a saint. *(page 68)*

chastity: The virtue by which people are able to successfully and healthfully integrate their sexuality into their total person; recognized as one of the fruits of the Holy Spirit. *(page 155)*

Christology: Literally the study of Christ; the systematic statement of Christian beliefs about Jesus Christ, including his identity, mission, and saving work on earth. *(page 29)*

Church Fathers: Teachers and writers in the early Church, many of whom were bishops, whose teachings are a witness to the Apostolic Tradition. *(page 27)*

circumcision: The act, required by Jewish law, of removing the foreskin of the penis. Since the time of Abraham, it has been a sign of God's Covenant relationship with the Jewish people. *(page 103)*

cloistered: Adjective indicating a religious order whose members rarely leave the monastery or convent that is their home. *(page 77)*

collects: Prayers offered by the person leading an assembly in communal prayer. *(page 97)*

conscience: A person's God-given internal sense of what is morally right or wrong. To make good judgments, a person needs to have a well-formed conscience. *(page 138)*

consecrate: Having made a person, place, or thing holy. The Consecration at Mass occurs during the Eucharistic Prayer, when the priest recites Jesus' words of institution, changing the bread and wine into the Body and Blood of Christ. *(page 126)*

covenant: A personal, solemn promise of faithful love that involves mutual commitments, such as the sacred agreement between God and his people. In the Old Covenant, God revealed his Law through Moses and prepared his people for salvation. He established a new and eternal Covenant in Jesus Christ, his only Son. *(page 11)*

D

divine economy: Also known as the economy of salvation, this refers to God's eternal plan and his actions for the salvation of humanity. *(page 13)*

doctrine: An official, authoritative teaching of the Church based on the Revelation of God. *(page 11)*

E

Ecumenical Council: A worldwide gathering of Catholic bishops convened by the Pope to discuss and resolve issues and problems the Church is facing. *(page 27)*

ecumenism: The movement to restore unity among all Christians, a unity that is a gift of Christ and to which the Church is called by the Holy Spirit. *(page 67)*

embryo: The unborn child from the time it implants in the uterine wall through the eighth week of its development. *(page 158)*

Eucharistic species: The gifts of bread and wine after they have become Christ's Body and Blood. *(page 125)*

evangelical counsels: The call to go beyond the minimum rules of life required by God (such as the Ten Commandments and the precepts of the Church) and strive for spiritual perfection through a life marked by a commitment to chastity, poverty, and obedience. *(page 131)*

Evangelists: Based on a word for "good news," in general, anyone who actively works to spread the Gospel of Jesus; more commonly and specifically, the persons traditionally recognized as authors of the four Gospels, Matthew, Mark, Luke, and John. *(page 62)*

evangelization: The proclamation of the Gospel of Jesus Christ through word and witness. *(page 221)*

F

Fall, the: Also called the Fall from Grace, the biblical revelation about the origins of sin and evil in the world, expressed figuratively in the story of Adam and Eve in Genesis. *(page 148)*

fetus: The unborn child from the end of the eighth week after conception to the moment of birth. *(page 158)*

filial: Having to do with the relationship of a child to his or her parents. *(page 17)*

free will: The gift from God that allows us to choose between good and evil. Human freedom attains its perfection when directed toward God. It is the basis for moral responsibility. *(page 53)*

G

genocide: The systematic and planned extermination of an entire national, racial, or ethnic group. *(page 157)*

Gentile: Someone who is not Jewish. *(page 58)*

grace: The gift of God's loving presence with us, which empowers us to respond to his call and to live always as his children. Grace is never earned; although none of us truly deserves grace, God freely chooses to bless us with this gift. *(page 121)*

H

Heaven: A state of eternal life and union with God, in which one experiences full happiness and the satisfaction of the deepest human longings. *(page 166)*

holy day of obligation: Feast day in the liturgical year on which, in addition to Sundays, Catholics are obliged to participate in the Eucharist. *(page 90)*

hypostatic union: The union of Jesus Christ's divine and human natures in one Divine Person. *(page 109)*

I

immortal: Living forever; not subject to death. *(page 149)*

incarnate: Having become flesh; specifically, God the Son assuming human nature. The Incarnation means that Jesus, the Son of God and Second Person of the Trinity, is both fully God and fully human. *(page 15)*

inspired: Written by human beings with the guidance of the Holy Spirit to teach without error those truths necessary for our salvation. *(page 58)*

intercessory prayer: A prayer form in which you ask God's help for other people's needs; also called intercession. *(page 200)*

interreligious dialogue: The Church's efforts to build relations with *other world religions*, such as Judaism and Islam. *(page 67)*

L

laity: All members of the Church with the exception of those who are ordained as bishops, priests, or deacons. The laity share in Christ's role as priest, prophet, and king, witnessing to God's love and power in the world. *(page 227)*

lament: A prayer, petition, or ritual of grief that honors the death of a loved one. Many of the psalms are examples of lament recorded in the Bible. *(page 189)*

Last Judgment: The judgment of the human race by Jesus Christ at his second coming, as noted in the Nicene Creed. It is also called the Final Judgment. *(page 21)*

litanies: Prayers consisting of a series of invocations and responses. *(page 209)*

liturgy: All official public prayer of the Church, including celebrations of the Eucharist and other Sacraments and the Liturgy of the Hours, the official daily prayers of the Church. *(page 124)*

M

Magisterium: The official, authoritative teaching voice of the Church. *(page 64)*

martyrs: People who suffer death because of their beliefs. The Church has canonized many martyrs as saints. *(page 51)*

Messiah: Hebrew word for "anointed one." The equivalent Greek term is *christos*. Jesus is the Christ and the Messiah because he is the Anointed One. *(page 22)*

missionaries: Those people who devote themselves to spreading the Gospel—in word and service—to those who have not heard it or to those who have rejected it; missionaries often serve in foreign countries. *(page 223)*

monotheism: The belief in and worship of only one God. *(page 12)*

N

Nicene Creed: The formal statement or profession of faith commonly recited during the Eucharist. *(page 12)*

noncanonical: Writings that are not part of a canon. *(page 63)*

novenas: From the Latin word for "nine," they are public or private devotions that extend for a period of nine days. *(page 209)*

O

Original Sin: The sin by which the first humans disobeyed God and thereby lost their original holiness and became subject to death. Original Sin is transmitted to every person born into the world, except Mary and Jesus. *(page 91)*

P

parables: Stories rooted in daily life that use symbolism or allegory as a teaching tool and that usually have a surprise ending. *(page 142)*

Parousia: The second coming of Christ, when his Kingdom will be fully established and his triumph over evil will be complete. *(page 183)*

patriarchs: The ancient fathers of the Jewish people, whose stories are recounted in the Book of Genesis. *(page 45)*

Pentecost: In Sacred Scripture, the event in which the early followers of Jesus received the Holy Spirit. Today the Church celebrates this event on Pentecost Sunday, which occurs seven weeks after Easter Sunday. *(page 23)*

personal sin: Any deliberate offense, in thought, word, or deed, against the will of God. *(page 91)*

Pharisees: A Jewish sect at the time of Jesus known for its strict adherence to the Law. *(page 104)*

philosophy: In Greek this word literally means "love of wisdom." It refers to the study of human existence using logical reasoning. *(page 27)*

pluralistic: Characterized by the presence of many different ethnic, religious, or cultural groups. *(page 107)*

prayer of petition: A prayer form in which you ask God for something you need. *(page 200)*

procreation: Conceiving and bearing children. *(page 155)*

Purgatory: A state of final purification or cleansing, which one may need to enter following death and before entering Heaven. *(page 167)*

R

Reign of God: The reign or rule of God over the hearts of people and, as a consequence of that, the development of a new social order based on unconditional love. The fullness of God's Reign will not be realized until the end of time. Also called the Kingdom of God. *(page 53)*

S

Sacraments: Efficacious and visible signs of God's invisible grace, instituted by Christ. The Seven Sacraments are Baptism, the Eucharist, Confirmation, Penance and Reconciliation, Anointing of the Sick, Matrimony, and Holy Orders. *(page 121)*

Sadducees: A Jewish sect at the time of Jesus known for its strong commitment to the Temple in Jerusalem. *(page 104)*

salvation history: The pattern of specific events in human history in which God clearly reveals his presence and saving actions. Salvation was accomplished once and for all through Jesus Christ, a truth foreshadowed and revealed throughout the Old Testament. *(page 42)*

Samaritans: Residents of Samaria, the central hill country of Palestine. In the time of Jesus, tremendous ethnic hatred and tension, which sometimes erupted into violence, existed between Jews and Samaritans. *(page 140)*

sanctifies: Makes holy; sanctification is the process of becoming closer to God and growing in holiness. *(page 101)*

sanctifying grace: A supernatural gift of God by which our sins are forgiven, we are made holy, and our friendship with God is restored. *(page 165)*

scribes: Jewish government officials and scholars of the Law. *(page 104)*

solemnities: Important holy days in the Catholic liturgical calendar, such as Christmas, Easter, Pentecost, and All Saints' Day. *(page 34)*

solidarity: Union of one's heart and mind with all people. Solidarity leads to the just distribution of material goods, creates bonds between opposing groups and nations, and leads to the spread of spiritual goods such as friendship and prayer. *(page 184)*

stewards: People who are put in charge of managing, caring for, and protecting something, such as money or personal property. *(page 143)*

synoptic Gospels: The Gospels of Mark, Matthew, and Luke are called *synoptic*—a word meaning "seen together"—because they appear to have been written using similar sources. *(page 178)*

T

theological virtues: The name for the God-given virtues of faith, hope, and love. These virtues make us open to living in a relationship with the Holy Trinity and are the foundation of the Christian moral life, animating it and giving it a special character. *(page 188)*

theology: Literally, "the study of God"; the academic discipline and effort to understand, interpret, and order our experience of God and Christian faith. *(page 81)*

Tradition: This word (from the Latin, meaning "to hand on") refers to the process of passing on the Gospel message. Tradition, which began with the oral communication of the Gospel by the Apostles, was written down in Scripture, is handed down and lived out in the life of the Church, and is interpreted by the Magisterium under the guidance of the Holy Spirit. *(page 64)*

Trinity: The truth that God, although one, is three Divine Persons: the Father, the Son, and the Holy Spirit. *(page 11)*

V

vocation: A calling from God to fulfill a particular purpose or mission in life. *(page 45)*

vows: Promises made to God. *(page 132)*

Index

Acknowledgments

The scriptural quotations in this book are from the *New American Bible with Revised New Testament and Revised Psalms*. Copyright © 1991, 1986, and 1970 by the Confraternity of Christian Doctrine, Washington, D.C. Used by the permission of the copyright owner. All Rights Reserved. No part of the *New American Bible* may be reproduced in any form without permission in writing from the copyright owner.

The excerpts marked *Catechism* and *CCC* are from the English translation of the *Catechism of the Catholic Church* for use in the United States of America, second edition. Copyright © 1994 by the United States Catholic Conference, Inc.—Libreria Editrice Vaticana. English translation of the *Catechism of the Catholic Church: Modifications from the Editio Typica* copyright © 1997 by the United States Catholic Conference, Inc.—Libreria Editrice Vaticana. Used with the permission of the USCCB.

The definitions in this book are taken from *The Catholic Faith Handbook for Youth*, second edition (Winona, MN: Saint Mary's Press, 2008), copyright © 2008 by Saint Mary's Press; *Saint Mary's Press® Essential Bible Dictionary*, by Sheila O'Connell-Roussell (Winona, MN: Saint Mary's Press, 2005), copyright © 2005 by Saint Mary's Press; and *Saint Mary's Press® Glossary of Theological Terms*, by John T. Ford (Winona, MN: Saint Mary's Press, 2006), copyright © 2006 by Saint Mary's Press. All rights reserved.

The excerpts on pages 12, 67, and 105 are from *Declaration on the Relation of the Church to Non-Christian Religions* (*Nostra Aetate*, 1965), numbers 4, 3, 2, and 4, respectively, in *Vatican Council II: Constitutions, Decrees, Declarations*, Austin Flannery, general editor (Northport, NY: Costello Publishing Company, 1996). Copyright © 1996 by Reverend Austin Flannery, OP.

The excerpts on pages 14, 94, 97, 98, 149, 228, and 230 are from *The Roman Missal* © 2010, International Commission on English in the Liturgy (ICEL). English translation prepared by the ICEL. Used with permission of the ICEL.

The quotation on page 34 is from *General Instruction of the Roman Missal*, number 67, at *www.usccb.org/liturgy/current/revmissalisromanien.shtml*. Copyright © 2003 by the United States Catholic Conference, Washington, D.C. All rights reserved.

The excerpts on pages 42 and 46 are from *Dogmatic Constitution on Divine Revelation* (*Dei Verbum*, 1965), numbers 3 and 4, at *www.vatican.va/archive/hist_councils/ii_vatican_council/documents/vat-ii_const_19651118_dei-verbum_en.html*.

The excerpts on pages 47, 62, 64, and 65 are from *Dogmatic Constitution on Divine Revelation* (*Dei Verbum*, 1965), numbers 3, 19, 18, 9, 10, and 9, respectively, in *Vatican Council II: Constitutions, Decrees, Declarations*, Austin Flannery, general editor (Northport, NY: Costello Publishing Company, 1996). Copyright © 1996 by Reverend Austin Flannery, OP.

The quotations on page 51 are from *Blessed Maximilian, OFM Conv.: Priest Hero of a Death Camp*, by Mary Craig (London: Catholic Truth Society, 1973).

The excerpts on pages 66, 213, 214, and 221 are from *Dogmatic Constitution on the Church* (*Lumen Gentium*, 1964), numbers 20, 59, 69, 55, and 35, respectively, in *Vatican Council II: Constitutions, Decrees, Declarations*, Austin Flannery, general editor (Northport, NY: Costello Publishing Company, 1996). Copyright © 1996 by Reverend Austin Flannery, OP.

The excerpts on pages 67 and 118 are from *Decree on Ecumenism* (*Unitatis Redintegratio*, 1964), number 3, in *Vatican Council II: Constitutions, Decrees, Declarations*, Austin Flannery, general editor (Northport, NY: Costello Publishing Company, 1996). Copyright © 1996 by Reverend Austin Flannery, OP.

The Prayer for Unity on page 68 is from "Pontifical Council for Promoting Christian Unity of Prayer," at *www.vatican.va/roman_curia/pontifical_councils/chrstuni/weeks-prayer-doc/rc_pc_chrstuni_doc_20070710_week-prayer-2008_en.html*.

The excerpts on pages 91 and 129 are from *Dogmatic Constitution on the Church* (*Lumen Gentium*, 1964), numbers 53 and 25, at *www.vatican.va/archive/hist_councils/ii_vatican_council/documents/vat-ii_const_19641121_lumen-gentium_en.html*.

The excerpt on page 94 is from *Declaration on the Relation of the Church to Non-Christian Religions* (*Nostra Aetate*, 1965), number 4, at *www.vatican.va/archive/hist_councils/ii_vatican_council/documents/vat-ii_decl_19651028_nostra-aetate_en.html*.

The excerpts on pages 101, 138, 154, and 155 are from *Pastoral Constitution on the Church in the Modern World* (*Gaudium et Spes*, 1965), numbers 22, 15, 22, and 29, respectively, in *Vatican Council II: Constitutions, Decrees, Declarations,* Austin Flannery, general editor (Northport, NY: Costello Publishing Company, 1996). Copyright © 1996 by Reverend Austin Flannery, OP.

The excerpt on page 116 is from "Address of His Holiness Benedict XVI to the Members of the Roman Curia for the Traditional Exchange of Christmas Greetings," at *www.vatican.va/holy_father/benedict_xvi/speeches/2008/december/documents/hf_ben-xvi_spe_20081222_curia-romana_en.html* .

The excerpts on pages 126, 127, and 206 are from *Constitution on the Sacred Liturgy* (*Sacrosanctum Concilium*, 1963), numbers 7, 14, and 10, respectively, in *Vatican Council II: Constitutions, Decrees, Declarations,* Austin Flannery, general editor (Northport, NY: Costello Publishing Company, 1996). Copyright © 1996 by Reverend Austin Flannery, OP.

The prayers on pages 129–130 and 164 from the English translation of *Rite of Baptism for Children* © 1969, ICEL, numbers 62, 62, and 63, and the quotations on page 166 from *Order of Christian Funerals* © 1985, ICEL, numbers 36, 38, 35, and 37, are found in *The Rites of the Catholic Church,* volume 1, prepared by the ICEL, a Joint Commission of Catholic Bishops' Conferences (Collegeville, MN: Liturgical Press, 1990). Copyright © 1990 by The Order of St. Benedict, Collegeville, MN. Used with permission of the ICEL.

The quotation by Sr. Helen Prejean on page 141 is from her Web site, *www.prejean.org*.

The excerpts on pages 152 and 153 are from "Letter of His Holiness Pope John Paul II to Artists," number 1, at *www.vatican.va/holy_father/john_paul_ii/letters/documents/hf_jp-ii_let_23041999_artists_en.html*.

The excerpt on page 162 is from the "17th World Youth Day, Papal Welcoming Ceremony, Address by the Holy Father John Paul II, July 25, 2002," number 2, at *www.vatican.va/holy_father/john_paul_ii/speeches/2002/july/documents/hf_jp-ii_spe_20020725_wyd-address-youth_en.html***.**

The quotation by John Paul II on page 188 is from "General Audience," number 1, at *www.vatican.va/holy_father/john_paul_ii/audiences/2000/documents/hf_jp-ii_aud_20001122_en.html*.

The quotations by John Paul II on page 216 are from "We Remember: A Reflection on the Shoah," number 1, at *www.vatican.va/roman_curia/pontifical_councils/chrstuni/documents/rc_pc_chrstuni_doc_16031998_shoah_en.html,* and from the Holy See Press Office, "His Holiness John Paul II: Pontificate," at *www.vatican.va/news_services/press/documentazione/documents/santopadre_biografie/giovanni_paolo_ii_biografia_pontificato_en.html*.

The quotation on page 220 is from a John Paul II homily, at *www.vatican.va/holy_father/john_paul_ii/homilies/1982/documents/hf_jp-ii_hom_19820530_coventry_en.html*.

The excerpt on page 222 is from *Decree on the Apostolate of Lay People* (*Apostolicam Actuositatem,* 1965), number 6, in *Vatican Council II: Constitutions, Decrees, Declarations,* Austin Flannery, general editor (Northport, NY: Costello Publishing Company, 1996). Copyright © 1996 by Reverend Austin Flannery, OP.

The goals listed on page 222 are from *Go and Make Disciples: A National Plan and Strategy for Catholic Evangelization in the United States,* Tenth Anniversary edition, numbers 46, 53, and 56, at *www.usccb.org/evangelization/goandmake/ourgoals. shtml.* Copyright © 2002 United States Conference of Catholic Bishops. All rights reserved.

The quotation describing the purpose of Maryknoll missioners on page 223 is from *www.mission-education.org/who_maryknoll.htm.*

The quotations from Cardinal Bernardin on page 231 are from the *New York Times,* August 31, 1996, at *query.nytimes.com/gst/fullpage.html?sec=health&res=9E0 4E2D61738F932A0575BC0A960958260&scp=2&sq=cardinal%20bernardin&st=cse.*

The excerpt from Pope Benedict XVI on page 233 is from "Encyclical Letter *Spe Salvi* of the Supreme Pontiff Benedict XVI to the Bishops, Priests and Deacons, Men and Women Religious, and All the Lay Faithful on Christian Hope," number 48, at *www.vatican.va/holy_father/benedict_xvi/encyclicals/documents/ hf_ben-xvi_enc_20071130_spe-salvi_en.html.*

To view copyright terms and conditions for Internet materials cited here, log on to the home pages for the referenced Web sites.

During this book's preparation, all citations, facts, figures, names, addresses, telephone numbers, Internet URLs, and other pieces of information cited within were verified for accuracy. The authors and Saint Mary's Press staff have made every attempt to reference current and valid sources, but we cannot guarantee the content of any source, and we are not responsible for any changes that may have occurred since our verification. If you find an error in, or have a question or concern about, any of the information or sources listed within, please contact Saint Mary's Press.

Endnotes Cited in Quotations from the *Catechism of the Catholic Church,* Second Edition

Section 1
1. Cf. *Isaiah* 66:13; *Psalm* 131:2.
2. St. Athanasius, *De inc.*, 54, 3: J. P. Migne, ed., Patrologia Graeca (Paris 1857–1866) 25, 192B.
3. Council of Chalcedon (451): Denzinger-Schonmetzer, *Enchiridion Symbolorum, definitionum et declarationum de rebus fidei et morum* (1965) 301; cf. *Hebrews* 4:15.
4. Cf. *Gaudium et spes* 25 § 1.

Section 2
1. *Roman Missal*, Good Friday 13: General Intercessions, VI.
2. St. Anselm, *Prosl. Prooem.*: J. P. Migne, ed., Patrologia Latina (Paris: 1841–1855) 153, 225A.
3. Vatican Council I, *Dei Filius* 2: Denzinger-Schonmetzer, *Enchiridion Symbolorum, definitionum et declarationum de rebus fidei et morum* (1965) 3004; cf. 3026; Vatican Council II, *Dei Verbum* 6.
4. Cf. *Dei Verbum* 14.
5. *Dei Verbum* 10 § 2.
6. *Lumen gentium* 25; cf. Vatican Council I: Denzinger-Schonmetzer, *Enchiridion Symbolorum, definitionum et declarationum de rebus fidei et morum* (1965) 3074.
7. *Gaudium et spes* 36 § 1.
8. *Liturgy of St. John Chrysostom*, Anaphora.

Section 3
1. Cf. *Genesis* 13:8; 14:16; 29:15; etc.
2. Cf. *Proverbs* 8:1—9:6; *Sirach* 24.
3. St. Athanasius, *De inc.*, 54, 3: J. P. Migne, ed., Patrologia Graeca (Paris 1857–1866) 25, 192B.
4. Cf. *John* 14:9–10.
5. Cf. *Galatians* 4:4.
6. Cf. *Galatians* 4:4.
7. Council of Chalcedon: Denzinger-Schonmetzer, *Enchiridion Symbolorum, definitionum et declarationum de rebus fidei et morum* (1965) 302.
8. Council of Constantinople II (553): Denzinger-Schonmetzer, *Enchiridion Symbolorum, definitionum et declarationum de rebus fidei et morum* (1965) (DS) 432; cf. DS 424; Council of Ephesus, DS 255.
9. Cf. *Luke* 1:43; 2:11.
10. Cf. *1 John* 1:8–10.
11. *Lumen gentium* 25.

Section 4
1. *Gaudium et spes* 38; cf. *Romans* 15:5; *Philippians* 2:5.
2. Cf. *John* 13:15; *Luke* 11:1; *Matthew* 5:11–12.
3. Cf. *Centesimus annus* 37–38.
4. Cf. Council of Trent: Denzinger-Schonmetzer, *Enchiridion Symbolorum, definitionum et declarationum de rebus fidei et morum* (1965) 1511–1512.
5. *Gaudium et spes* 29 § 2.
6. Cf. *Genesis* 1:26.
7. Cf. *Gaudium et spes* 22.
8. Cf. *Genesis* 2:7, 22.
9. Congregation for the Doctrine of the Faith, *Donum Vitae* I, 3.
10. Cf. Council of Trent (1546): Denzinger-Schonmetzer, *Enchiridion Symbolorum, definitionum et declarationum de rebus fidei et morum* (1965) 3004; cf. 3026; Vatican Council II, *Dei Verbum* 1511.
11. *2 Corinthians* 5:17; *2 Peter* 1:4; cf. *Galatians* 4:5–7.
12. Cf. *1 Corinthians* 6:15; 12:27; *Romans* 8:17.
13. Cf. *1 Corinthians* 6:19.
14. *1 Corinthians* 2:9.
15. *2 Peter* 1:4; cf. *John* 17:3.
16. *Roman Catechism* 3, 2, 4.
17. Cf. *Isaiah* 58:6–7; *Hebrews* 13:3.
18. Cf. *Isaiah* 58:6–7; *Hebrews* 13:3.

Section 5
1. St. Thomas Aquinas, *Summa Theologiae* III, 65, 3.
2. Cf. *Lumen gentium* 48–50.
3. Cf. *Sollicitudo rei socialis* 1; 41.
4. *Lumen gentium* 35 § 1, § 2.
5. *Lumen gentium* 35 § 1, § 2.
6. Cf. *Mark* 16:16; *John* 3:36; 6:40 et al.
7. St. Augustine, *De civ. Dei*, 22, 30: J. P. Migne, ed., Patrologia Latina (Paris: 1841–1855) 41, 801–802; cf. *Leviticus* 26:12; cf. *1 Corinthians* 15:28.
8. *Indulgentiarum doctrina*, 5.
9. *Roman Missal*, Preface of Christian Death I.
10. Cf. *John* 3:18; 12:48; *Matthew* 12:32; *1 Corinthians* 3:12–15; *Hebrews* 6:4–6; 10:26–31.